Love
Finds a *Way*

A story of just one day and the events
of that day in a family where
putting Christ first counts . . .

Dewey Painter

ISBN 978-1-64299-589-3 (paperback)
ISBN 978-1-64299-967-9 (hardcover)
ISBN 978-1-64299-590-9 (digital)

Copyright © 2018 by Dewey Painter

All rights reserved. No part of this publication may be reproduced, distributed, or transmitted in any form or by any means, including photocopying, recording, or other electronic or mechanical methods without the prior written permission of the publisher. For permission requests, solicit the publisher via the address below.

Christian Faith Publishing, Inc.
832 Park Avenue
Meadville, PA 16335
www.christianfaithpublishing.com

Printed in the United States of America

To my wife of fifty-two years, Clara Painter.

Inspiration

As a young Christian I was given a book called *In His Steps* by Shelton. This book was an absolute blessing and guide for me. It helped me to shape my life by doing all that I attempted with first asking, "How would Jesus do this or have me do it?" Over the years I purchased hundreds of copies of the book and gave them to new believers or believers who needed direction in their lives with the hope that it would inspire them as it did me.

The book is very hard to find today, but with some research it can be found. There was never a sequel to the book written that I know of. While recovering from a major operation and having time to use my mind and computer, I felt led to write this book but with it portraying the life of an average Christian family for just one day. What a day differences can make in our lives and when others and love is put forth first then a way can be found for every circumstance.

This book is fictional, however the experiences I have had over the past fifty-seven years as a Christian and over half of those years in service for the Lord influenced me to develop the characters in this writing. I trust that you will enjoy reading this book and that perhaps it will inspire you in your service for the Lord.

Chapter 1

It was a clear early spring morning with heavy dew across the grass fields. It had the appearance of a light snow, and it glittered like glass as the sun rose, and then it slowly began to dissipate. This was one of those lazy hazy mornings when Jay wished he could just lay in bed, close his eyes, and go back to sleep. However, reality set in, and he knew that he would have to rise and face the day.

While he waited for a surge of energy, which hopefully would strengthen his ability to get up, his mind wandered over the things that he must accomplish during the day. The list seemed to be endless as he found himself mentally placing his thoughts in some order of mental priority within his mind. At times like this, he wished he would have had the foresight the night before to lay a tablet and pencil beside his bed. It certainly would help him to remember that perfect order he had finally arranged his priorities. Prior to getting up, Jay knew the most important need of the day, the one thing that is absolute to his being successful this day, the one thing that allows his confidence to have real assurance, and that one thing was prayer.

In the freshness of the morning, Jay began to put his thoughts and burdens before the Lord. In his mind he was saying, *Lord, I thank you for who you are and what you have done in my life. I thank you for loving me, saving me, and using me. I thank you for the opportunities that you have given me to serve you, and I thank you for this day. Lord, as I begin my day, let me do it with you. As I walk the steps of this day, I pray that your Spirit will guide me. Let my direction be your direction, let my speech be your speech, and let my character exemplify you in all that I do. You have chosen me for the task of serving you; I would not have picked me for I know that I am not worthy or adequate, yet you selected me. I thank you for this and now ask that where I lack wisdom, you will show me wisdom; where I lack strength, you will give me strength; and where I lack determination, you will keep me steadfast to the tasks before me. I pray for my family that they will put Christ first in their lives and will look to you for guidance in all that they do. I pray for my fellow workers that you will meet each of their needs; and I pray these things in the precious name of our Lord and Savior, Jesus Christ. Amen.*

Having completed his morning thoughts and prayers, Jay rolled over and off the bed. As his feet touched the smooth waxed hard wood floor, they jumped back up from the chill he felt. *Must I do this*, he thought. And as if he felt he needed a verbal answer, he spoke out, "Yes! It is time to begin the day and do that which the Lord has for me to do." So with new courage, he placed his feet on the floor and arose. With a quick pace, he entered the bathroom for daily preparation. The hot shower and shave felt good. With a dash of after-shave lotion and a spot of deodorant or two, he headed back into the bedroom to find the closet and his clothes for the day. As he selected his clothes, he noticed a Blue Jay as it landed on a branch of the tree outside his bedroom window. The Blue Jay sat with its head erect and surveyed all that was around him. Jay thought that this was a good parallel for him, his name was Jay and he had just finished surveying the needs of the day which were before him; he also remembered his mother had named him after the Blue Jay. To her it was one of the most wonderful things God had made. His last name was Washington. He often bragged that he was a direct descendant of the first president of the United States, George Washington. As he told the story, President George Washington was one of his great-great-great-grandfathers. He had never traced his lineage, so if asked he would simply say, "Well, that's what my mama told me." Clearing his thoughts, as the Blue Jay flew away, perhaps in search of the first task of the day, he knew that was his time to do the same thing.

He quickly dressed in casual work clothes. Today was a workday, requiring manual labor and his usual dress shirt and tie just would not do. He finished dressing, giving a quick look into the mirror as he started to leave the room. He suddenly stopped. He had taken all the effort and steps to properly present himself today, and as more usual than he would like to admit, he had once again forgotten to comb his hair it looked like an explosion in a mattress factory. Grabbing his hairbrush, he quickly brushed his hair as he chuckled at the sight of it. Having done this final task, he was now ready to descend the steps and begin the day. His thoughts suddenly went to the emptiness in his stomach as he smelled fresh cooking bacon. It seemed to extend to every room of the house and also entered into his nostrils. He loved that smell and hoped it was the thick country style that he loved, and which he knew was not best for him to eat. Descending the steps, he was met at the bottom by his faithful, loving dog.

For some reason, he had chosen to name the dog George. When asked why, he would reply by saying, "When I got him I thought of what most folks say about dogs, being man's best friend. One of the best friends I have ever had was a service buddy named George." He and George had been on the battlefield together and had saved each other's lives several times. *George would not mind*, Jay thought, *in fact he would encourage it*. After the war, they both came home; however, a drunk driver killed George a few years ago. What a tragedy! Here was a man that fought for his country; won the Silver Star and a host of other decorations, including the Purple Heart; he had gone through all that to lose his life to a senseless act of a man who had a drinking problem, had several DUI convictions, and was still driving.

George had stopped to change a flat tire when this drunk plowed into the back of his car, hitting George and killing him instantly. At least he did not suffer. And besides, who wants a dog with the common names most folks give them? George had been my best friend, and they say that a dog is man's best friend, so it was only fitting that I call him George, I know George would approve if he were here.

The dog had a golden color with strong muscle tones and for his two years of life, he had grown into a find beautiful specimen of a golden Labrador. He was keen in his thinking and strong in his determination. He could look at you seriously, making you wonder what he was really going to do. And most importantly, was he going to do it to you. He usually broke that exterior look with a tail that wagged briskly back and forth, with a bark and a few playful bounces, which made you realized that he had once again accepted you and welcomed you. George was a good name for him, for my friend George had all of these redeeming qualities. As he hugged and patted the dog, the smell of the bacon brought him back to reality, and he realized that he must enter the dining room if he were to ever taste of that wonderful smell.

As he entered the room, he saw Nell, his wonderful wife of twenty years, skipping around the kitchen with the ease of a ballet dancer, carefully taking each step as her mind and actions played out the task of getting breakfast ready for her family. This was the time of the day that Nell loved best. She had her family to herself, and they were focused on the results of what she was doing for them, not because of some sense of duty or as a chore. With every step, every flip of the flapjacks, every cracking of an egg, and the pouring of the milk and coffee, she was expressing her love to them. Of course it helped greatly that they loved her cooking. This was something she assumed, for they always quickly ate all that she prepared, seldom was a scrap left. If George was to be fed from the drippings or left over from the table, he would not survive. Coming up behind Nell, Jay circled his arms around her, and as he hugged her, he gently kissed her just below her right ear lope and then gave it a little nip.

"Ouch!" Nell said. "Breakfast is on the table, not standing in my shoes," she exclaimed with that special little chirp and cheerful voice, which always assured Jay that she really liked the attention. "Breakfast is served," Nell spoke into the intercom system, which went to every room of the house. *What a neat device,* she thought, *sure saves my lungs and overcomes the excuse, "I didn't hear you."*

With a sound as if a train was coming through the house, each of the children entered the room. Billy, their oldest son who was twelve; June, their sweet summer rose who was almost eleven; and last but not least, here comes Patrick Henry who was five. Patrick Henry liked his full name and was quick to let you know you were not calling him or speaking to him if you only called one of his names. *I am sure he will be much worse after he hears about a patriot of many years ago by the same name,* thought Nell. Each of the children had their assigned sitting place. Nell came from a large family and now understood why her mother had such a rule. Billy was the first to find his seat as he jumped into it and then tried to move it forward, you could hear it scrape the floor as he pulled it across the wood floor. "Billy," his father called out, "please do not pull your chair in that way, it messes up the nice floor your mother so dearly loves and cares for."

"Sorry," Billy said, "I saw all the good food Mom had on the table and forgot myself."

"Flattery will get you past me," said Mom.

Patrick Henry was usually the first at his seat. As he climbed up into his chair, he gave Billy a commanding look. "I would have been first if you have not gotten in front of me on the stairs and held me back," exclaimed Patrick Henry.

"Sorry, kid," said Billy, "but I could smell that Mom was cooking my favorite today, and I guess that it just overcame me."

"Well, it's just not right! You should have to go back upstairs and start all over again," said Patrick Henry, "and don't call me kid either."

Mom stood between the boys, she hugged them both and said, "Fussing children, don't eat at my table." Both boys quickly dropped the subject and proceeded to prepare themselves for the meal.

"June, I can see that you are here for breakfast, but it is customary to sit down to eat, unless you are starting a new trend in breakfast methods," said Dad.

"Oh, Dad, I was just thinking about what it would be like to have a sister instead of two brothers!" With a sigh after having made such an expression, she quickly took her seat.

Dad was already seated and was waiting on Mom to join them at the table. "You go ahead, dear," sang out Nell. "I'll join you shortly."

"Thanks, but we can wait for you. This is breakfast, but it is also our sweetest family time, which needs you to make it complete," said Jay. With that challenge, Nell took her seat.

As was their custom, each morning the family gathered around the table for family devotions. Before the meal, their thoughts were quick and direct; this helped to eat the food while it was still hot, and after the meal, they had their daily Bible reading and thoughts.

"June, since you were the last one at the table today, we will let you pray," said Dad.

"I was not the last, Mom was," quickly replied June.

"Mom was here already getting our breakfast ready, so that doesn't count, so pray," said Dad with that direct and meaningful voice of his. He was concerned about June; she tried to avoid many responsibilities, especially spiritual ones. This was certainly a matter for prayer and seeking of the Lord's direction on speaking to June about her attitude and lack of spiritual concern.

"Dear Lord," prayed June, "we ask that you bless this food and this house and Mom's hard work for breakfast, Amen." *Short and direct*, thought Dad, *but a meaningful prayer*.

The boys both said at the same time, "Good work, June! Short so we can eat." And eat they did. The Lord had blessed by providing the food needs for the Washington family, for which they were thankful.

Each of the boys made a stack of flapjacks on their plates, one trying to out-stack the other. Mom interceded by saying, "Remember you have to eat what you take, and from my view, I believe you boys have eyes that are much bigger than your stomach."

The boys settled on having just three apiece, Dad took four, and Mom and June took two apiece. Beside the flapjacks, there were scrambled eggs and some good country thick sliced bacon and a few sausage patties. June and Mom took the sausage patties. Dad and the boys shared the bacon.

"You boys slow down eating, you are not going to a fire or a race," said Mom in her authoritative voice, the one she used when she wanted the children to understand she meant what she was saying.

"Ah, Mom, we are not eating that fast! Besides the food is so good, I want to eat it all up before it gets cold," said Billy.

"No excuses," said Mom, "just slow down!" Which they did. There was some small talk over the events of yesterday and of the anticipation of today, but no real conversation to repeat.

They were all busy enjoying the meal that Mom had made for them. As the mealtime came to a close, Dad took his Bible and said, "OK, boys, it's your turn to clear the table, do it quickly so we can finish our devotions."

"But—" said Billy, intending to object to doing the clearing, however, Dad interrupted before he could say any more. "No buts," said Dad. "Remove the dishes off the table and please do it quickly and quietly."

June chuckled and thought to herself, *The boys really got put in their place today; if it were up to me I would have them do the clearing for a whole month.* She thought this, not out of fairness, but because she didn't want to do the clearing either.

With the table cleared and everyone sitting back down to hear the devotions, Dad began by reading in the first chapter of Romans. He read a few verses and then stopped to explain what the verses were saying. "In verse one," Dad said, "the Apostle Paul had identified himself as a servant. What does that mean, Patrick Henry?"

"That he serves," was Patrick Henry's quick reply.

"Could you be a little more specific?" said Dad.

"Well," began Patrick Henry, "Paul loved the Lord so much he wanted to serve Him."

"That's better and closer to the meaning," said Dad. "The Apostle Paul often identified himself as a servant of the Lord or a prisoner of the Lord. This was used to explain the detail to which he was committed to the Lord. By being a servant, it was like that of being a bond slave; he was totally committed to his master to do the master's bidding without question, because he loved the master.

"Because Paul loved the Lord, he wanted to serve Him," as Patrick Henry suggested. "If we love the Lord, then we will want to serve Him also. Not just in our home life, but at school, play, or work. Our lives should be committed to the Lord so that others can see Christ in us. We can gather much from today's lesson, now let's pray and then go and make application of what we have seen from God's Word today. Who would like to pray for us today?" asked Dad.

"I would," Billy quickly replied.

"OK then, you pray."

"Jesus," Billy began his prayer, "we do love you and want to serve you. We ask that you help us this day to do all that you want us to do to show our love for you. Bless each one of us as we go to our appointed places, in Jesus's name, Amen."

"What does he mean appointed places?" piped up Patrick Henry.

"Each of us has a place to go today," replied Mom. "You children must go to your individual classes at school, Dad must go to his work, and I must be busy about my work here at home—these are our appointed places."

With the morning devotions completed, everyone got ready to leave for their appointed places, except Mom. She got to stay since she was already at her appointed place. The boys raced June to the bus stop; and Dad, giving Nell a quick kiss goodbye, got into his car and drove off to work.

Chapter 2

As Jay drove down the street, he began to think of all work that he needed to do today. He began to put into mental priority the things which he needed to accomplish. One of his coworkers, Bill Wilson, usually rode to work with him, so Jay headed to Bill's house to pick him up. They usually took turns driving, one month at a time. This helped expenses and made the forty-minute ride more enjoyable. As Jay's thoughts went to Bill, he began to pray for Bill. He had witnessed to Bill several times and had hopes of seeing him come to accept the Lord Jesus Christ as his personal Savior. Bill had been receptive, yet had many difficulties in accepting Christ. This may have been in part because of some earlier incidents in his life as a young boy. He had shared a little about the difficulties with Jay before. With just brief details of a life-changing event earlier in Bill's life, the details helped Jay to understand that his task was to share his testimony and God's Word and then let the Holy Spirit do the convincing. Bill needed a real encounter with Christ, not an easy "believism." Just as Jay finished his prayer for Bill, he pulled into Bill's driveway and tooted the horn.

Bill came out on the first toot, which was unusual; usually Jay had to go and knock on the door and almost wake him up to get him going. Bill jumped in the car and said, "Let's go." As Jay backed into the street and headed toward the workplace, he said to Bill, "We certainly are quick this morning! What got you up so early and raring to go?"

"Something happened to me last night, which I am sure you will be happy to hear." He hesitated for a few moments as if collecting his thoughts and being sure of his words, but moments seemed like minutes, so Jay spoke up first, "Well, come on, out with it! What's got you so fired up this morning?"

"Over the weekend, I went up state to visit my folks, and while I was there I met a girl that I knew in high school, her name was Mary. I really had a crush on her in high school but was afraid to let her know it. I found out that she was still single and had let my folks know she was glad I was able to come home for the weekend and hoped that finally I would call on her. This was a dream come true, I am sure that she did not expect my folks to tell me just exactly what she said, but they did. I called her Saturday afternoon and asked if we could go out for dinner that evening. She said yes! Wow! Was I on cloud nine? I thought she never even noticed me.

"It was almost seven o'clock when I picked her up for dinner. I came to the door, where her dad met me. It was good to see her folks again. After a brief conversation, we left for dinner.

"She was more beautiful than I remembered in high school, and there was something peculiarly sweet about her that I had not noticed before. I wasn't sure what it was, but it sure made her more of a mystery to me than ever before.

"We went to a French restaurant and had a wonderful meal. I thought it odd that she only drank water instead of the wine offered by the waiter. I was not sure why, so I ordered tea for myself.

"As we sat at the table, I could barely keep from asking her about what was so different about her. I shared with her that I really liked her during high school, which she said she had noticed and often wondered why I never asked her out. I said, 'I guess it was because I was shy and was afraid you would say no. I don't believe I could have handled your rejection if you did.' The more we talked, the more the mystery of her beauty built up, and I just had to ask her. 'Mary,' I said, 'there is something extra different about you, which almost makes you glow; please forgive my frankness, but what is it? What happened to you that made you even sweeter than I remember you in high school?'

"'Bill,' she began, 'the first couple of years after high school my life was very difficult. I had a good family and home, I even found a good job, but I just did not seem to have any joy until September of last year when something wonderful happened in my life. She hesitated for a moment as if she was searching for the right words. After what seemed to be minutes, but in reality was only moments, she said, 'Bill, last September I became a Christian, I accepted the Lord Jesus Christ as my personal Savior, and now I have real joy and peace such as I have never known before. I wasn't aware that it showed so much for you to notice, but I am glad that you did, for I wanted to share with you and with others what Christ has done for me. Bill, are you a Christian?' Mary asked. 'Well, not really,' I replied. 'Jay is one of my coworkers and we ride to work together each day, he's been talking to me about it, but I was not ready for religion.' 'Neither was I,' said Mary, 'I didn't want religion, and I wanted something that was real. I found that reality in Jesus, being a Christian is the best thing that has ever happened to me, and I would like for you to know Christ also.'

"I was not prepared or ready for the open frankness of what Mary had to say. I was confused because I had tried so hard to put any thoughts about religion or church behind me. With little hesitation from Mary, I changed the subject back to talking about our high school days and what we had done since then. While Mary did not push the subject, it did come up briefly during the evening. She still retained her sweet spirit, made her previous words and the mystery of her sink even more into my thoughts.

"As the night passed, I listened intently to all that Mary had to say, at first I thought maybe I had better go along with her on this or I may not be able to see her again, then I realized that would be wrong and for the wrong reason. Mary gently and kindly shared with me what had happened in her heart, and as she did so the Holy Spirit began to work in my heart. It seemed like hours had passed away and as I looked at my watch I noticed it was only half past eight. I tried to put my mind on other things, yet I could not. I remembered as a small boy I attended a Sunday school class and my teacher shared verses of the Scripture with the class. None of that had made sense until now, I found myself saying within me, 'I'm not sure what it is that Mary and Jay have, but I want it for my life also, but not now, I must think about these things.'

"At what seemed to be a mutual unspoken signal, we finished the rest of our dinner. After dinner we rode, mostly in silence as we drove back to her house. I pulled up into the driveway and got out to walk her to the door. As we stood in front of the door, I thanked her for the lovely evening and expressed how astonished I was that she really did go out with me. I also thanked her for sharing what had happened in her life. I felt that she had shared some deep secrets with me (I did not understand at the time that when you are Christian, you share with others all that Christ has done for you, as the opportunity presents itself.) I asked if I could see her again. She said she was hoping I would and asked if I could go to church with her Sunday morning. I was not ready for that question, as I had said I would never go to church again because of something that happened in my earlier years. She started to speak, yet let her question hang, waiting for my answer. I tried to think of excuses, but could not, so I said, 'Sure why not, what time do I pick you up?' 'About nine thirty would do fine,' she said. 'Nine thirty it is.'

"We exchanged a few more words, and I thought it would be appropriate to kiss her good night, but for some reason felt it would be forward of me. I think she understood my thoughts, reaching up she lightly kissed me on the cheek and slipped inside before I could respond. 'Wow, that's the first time that has ever happened to me, I hope this is something that is going to get serious,' I thought to myself. With new warmth in my heart, I left and went home.

"After visiting my folks for a while, I rose from the couch and headed toward my room to go to bed. 'By the way,' I said in passing, 'I am picking up Mary for church in the morning at nine thirty.' 'Wonder why she goes so early,' I thought as I closed the door behind me and went to my room. As I lay on the bed, I remembered the look in my folk's eyes and the expression on their face when I made the announcement about church the next day. You could have heard a pin drop as they both went completely silent, yet the wonderful smiles that came on their faces gave me the assurance of their approval and delight.

"I was really tired and wanted to get to sleep, but I could not sleep. I could not help but think of all that Mary and I had talked about on our date. She was so serious and sincere about her faith. I just could not believe it. In fact, as I thought about it, it reminded me about you, Jay. I knew she had the same kind of faith you had, and I wondered if I would ever find such faith, peace, and happiness. What seemed like hours, was not, and I drifted off to sleep.

"Awaking the next morning, I got up early, showered twice, shaved twice, put on smelling sauce twice, and combed my hair three or four times before breakfast. I put on the best clothes I had with me, which I felt were not adequate. I had not come prepared to go to church and had left all my suits at home. Mom must have read my thoughts, for just as I had tried on every set of clothes I had, she knocked on the door. I opened the door and hanging on the doorknob was a really good-looking dark suit with a note. *This was your uncle's, and he was about your size. Try it on and if it fits, it's yours.* I removed the plastic covering from the cleaners and quickly put the suit on. A tailor could not have given me a better fit. Having finished dressing, I left my room and went into the kitchen for breakfast, Mom had already called me twice.

"'Wow,' whistled Mom, 'who is this good-looking man in my house? Will you look at him, Dad? In that suit he looks just like your younger brother did twenty years ago.' Dad gave a warm smile and with what looked like a tear in his eye, a big hug. 'OK, you two,' Mom said, 'it's time to eat and for this boy to get off to pick up Mary. Son, we've decided to join you later if you don't mind.' 'They like crowds at the church, so come on,' I replied. I ate breakfast so quickly I cannot remember what I ate. Quite frankly, my mind was on picking up Mary.

"As I stood at the door waiting for someone to answer, the door suddenly opened without warning, and a little fellow, whom I assumed was Mary's little brother, said, 'Come on in, we were waiting for you. Mary said I could ride with you, is that OK?' 'Sure,' I said. In a few moments, Mary joined us. At first I could not believe my eyes. She was beautiful last night, but today she could have won any beauty contest she dared to enter. I was at a loss for words and was awakened from my thoughts as I heard her say, 'Bill, are you OK? Is everything all right?' 'Sure,' I said, 'I was just awestruck at how pretty you are this morning.' To which she blushed and said, 'We had best go.' She really wanted to change the subject.

"Going to church was the last thing I would ever think that I would be doing. As I drove toward the church, my mind was going over what happened to change my mind. Was it the girl? Perhaps it was the combined testimony of both Mary and Jay. Whatever it was, I was committed to be there and felt I should grow up a little and face the day. What harm could there be in my going, I never vowed to anybody I would not, I just always made the choice to say no, before.

"As I drove, my mind went back to the last time I had gone to church as a boy.

"My dad took the family to church, but it was understood that *all* went and there was really no vote or choice. At first I enjoyed going to Sunday school and while I did not understand the sermons much, I did like the music. As I entered into the sixth grade, a terrible thing happened to me. I had really come to trust my teacher, a man about in his forties. He was a kind man, and when he offered to take the class on a camping trip, we were all for it. We went to a lake way back in the woods where there was really no one; the road to the lake was just a small almost unused dirt path. After we set up camp, it was early in the afternoon and it was a hot summer day. The teacher said he thought we should all go swimming. 'But teacher,' said one of the boys, 'you didn't tell us we were going to a lake and go swimming, so no one brought swimsuits.' 'No problem,' the teacher said, 'we are all men here so we can swim in our undershorts or nothing, there are no girls around so we don't have to worry.' A number of us boys had slipped off to the creek before and went skinny-dipping, but never with an adult with us, and certainly not with all these other guys.

"Some of us must have done this with the teacher before, for they began to tease us, 'Don't you little boys want to come in the water, or are you sissys?' They had already taken off all their clothes and jumped into the water. We, remaining four boys, looked at each other as one said, 'Well, I guess it will be all right, but I'm leaving my shorts on!' So we all four did the same thing and after undressing, jumped into the water. I was not prepared for what happened. I have never seen an adult man naked and really did not want to see one, so I was really shocked when the teacher took off all his clothes and jumped into the water with us. We played some water games, like basketball using one of the inner tubes for the hoop. During the games there were times we bumped into each other and had water fights over the ball. However, it seemed that each time we had three or four close together, then hands would touch where they should not touch and I began to get very scared. I did not understand what was going on, but I knew this was not what a group of sixth grade Sunday school boys on a camp out should be doing.

"I made an excuse to leave the water, picked up my clothes, and went into the woods. After dressing, which I did very quickly, I walked away from the campsite. I was not sure where I was going; I just did not want to stay there. At first I felt maybe I was deserting my other friends, but found our later that my action caused a reaction, which prevented any further things from happening to them. After a while, they began to notice I was not back. They called my name; I was quite far from them and could barely hear them. One of the boys, Jimmy, told me later that the teacher began to get real nervous, and told all the boys to get out of the water, get dressed, and help him find me. They did this and looked for over an hour, but I evaded them. Now the teacher had two problems, he had lost one of his students and now he must go and seek help. I wondered if he knew why he had lost me, and what would happen when they found me!

"Now I had a problem, I had gotten myself lost in the woods. I wandered for hours, until it was pitch black dark. Every sound of the forest began to play on my imagination. They had notified the Forestry Service, since we were in a State Park area. There was a search party out looking for me, but I had covered so much ground, (on purpose,) that I was far beyond the search area they had set up. I was tired, cold, hungry, and hurting from the cuts and stings I received as I ran through the underbrush. Will I live? I wondered. Will anyone every find me? Maybe I was wrong in running away, maybe I should have just said, 'I don't like what's going on and I want it stopped.' As I wandered in the night, I saw a small light, which seemed to be miles away, near a hillside. I hoped it was a streetlight or a porch light. I began to make my way in that direction. After about two hours of painful effort, I found myself standing outside a small barn, which was inside a fenced field. There were no other houses or signs of life around, except for the barn. I slowly eased up to one of the side windows, wiped the dust off the glass, and with my heart pounding, I ventured to peek inside. There was an inside light on also, which I found out later was because the owner had forgotten to turn it off. I could see several horses and cows and a whole lot of hay, but no people. As I looked through the window, I began to realize how tired I was and felt that if the animals were safe, maybe I would be safe inside also.

"As my courage rose, I made my way around to the front of the barn. One of the two large doors to the barn had a smaller door, which I tried and found it to be unlocked. Carefully opening the door, I looked inside, and after feeling confidence that all was well, I entered the barn and closed the door behind me. I stood inside the door for a long time. This was a really neat place. I had seen pictures of places like this before, but I had never actually been in a barn before. My mind left my problems for a few minutes while I enjoyed the wonder of what I was seeing. I loved the smell of the hay, and I began to relax as I became acquainted with my surroundings, I returned to reality and remembered what had brought me there, and that I was tired and hungry. I knew there was food for the animals, but surely nothing there that I could eat; and then I spotted what looked to me to be a basket of apples, at the far end of the barn. With great hope I made my way to the end of the barn, carefully speaking to the animals in their stalls to assure them that I meant them no harm. To my wonderful delight, it was apples. They were not in very good shape and were to be given to the pigs the owner had on the backside of the barn—outside of course. As I separated though them, I picked out ones which I felt were solid enough to eat—some I could only eat half or just a bite. I had eaten several, which took away my stomach pains, when I noticed the horse nearest where I was was looking right at me! It seemed he was licking his chops and his eyes were begging for me to give an apple also. I did, and that was exactly what he wanted. I gave the other two horses some too. The cows seemed to care less.

"Sleep was upon me, and I could hardly hold my eyes open. I found a couple of blankets they used for the horses and made myself a bed on top of a big stack of hay. It only took a few moments for me to fall asleep. I was so tired I could have slept for days, and if someone had tried to get me during the night, I would not have heard them coming if I tried. As I began to wake the next day, the sun had found an open knothole and sent a beam of sunlight that played over my eyes as a beam from a flashlight. It almost woke me up, but what really woke me was the man standing over me saying, 'Boy, wake up, what are you doing in my barn?' He said this several times, but it took me a while to get beyond sleep and back to reality. As I realized I had been found out, I curled up in defense and said, 'Mister, please don't hurt me, I was lost and cold and hungry and needed somewhere to get out of the night.' As I said this, I began to cry.

"'Now, son, don't do that, I'm not going to hurt you or even touch you. My name is Cecil and I just thought I ought to know who's using my barn.' His voice came across with care and concern; as I looked into his face I could see the kindness in his eyes and I could tell by the sincerity in his voice that he meant me no harm. I sat up and told him I was sorry for entering his barn without permission, but I had no other place to go. 'Why don't you tell me the whole story, so I can better understand how you got way out here and into my barn,' he said. After a moment of thought, he handed me a sandwich and a can of soda. 'Why don't you have this first, and then you can tell me,' he said with the gentleness of a grandfather.

"While I ate the sandwich and drank the soda, he was busy tending to his animals in the barn. As I took the last bite, I said, 'Mr. Cecil, thank you for your kindness and for not being mean to me about being in your barn. Sir, your barn was a life saver to me,' I said with my voice picking up speed as I spoke. 'Slow down,' he said, 'tell me the whole story and I will see what I can do to help you from here.' As I thought about the events of the past day, I did not think I could say anything to anyone about it, it would be embarrassing, what if I had misunderstood what was going on? I could really hurt a lot of people, and maybe I was the one that had been wrong.

"'Well,' he said, 'are you going to speak or did my barn cat get your tongue?'" Mr. Cecil said in a cheerful voice. He seemed to sense I was in a lot of mental tremor and was trying to help me to relax.

"'I didn't see the cat,' I replied, 'and since you can hear me, he didn't get my tongue.'

"'Then tell me your tale,' he said.

"As I began to tell of the events of the past day, I tried to tell what I thought were the facts and to be sure I was not adding things to make my story sound better. As I spoke, a dark expression came over his face, and the more I spoke, the expression got darker. The face that just a few moments earlier was one that was smiling and happy, now was sad and had a hurting look to it. I was not sure and said, 'Should I go on?'

"'Yes, son, please do so. I am sad because of what you have had to go through and I feel I am beginning to understand your pain also. I know the lake you spoke of and perhaps I know of who it was that took you boys to the lake, but that's another matter, please continue,' he said with what seemed to be an urgent voice.

"I completed telling him all that I knew, why I had gotten out of the water, and ran away into the woods; and how I found his barn.

"After I finished, he sat and stared through the open barn door for a few moments, then with a kind voice he began to speak. 'Son, what is your name?' he asked.

"'Billy, but my friends call me Bill.'

"'Well, Bill, I want to be your friend, so if you don't mind I'll just call you Bill.'

"'That sounds great to me,' I said, for I had really begun to like this fellow, who reminded me of my grandfather.

"'Bill,' he said, 'we need to get some help and get this matter looked into. I am sure your folks are worried about you, and I do remember something on the radio news this morning, which I listen to each morning as I drive to this barn, about a boy being lost in the woods last night. Would you mind if I go to my truck and get my phone and bring it back here in the barn?'

"'You've got a phone in your truck and you can bring it with you wherever you go Wow! that's great,' I said. 'I want to see it, can I make a call on it too?'

"'Sure,' he said as he walked out the barn door and over to his truck. He came back in a few moments and said, 'Now we need to make at least two calls. I'll make the first one, and then you can make the second one. The sheriff is a personal friend of mine and I am going to call him at his home so that he can call off the search and come over here and help us, is that all right with you?'

"'Is that the right thing to do? Can't we just call my parents?'

"'The right thing for us to do, is both, agreed?'

"I had already learned to trust him and felt I should do as he asked.

"He made the first call and without going into a lot of details told the Sheriff what he had found in his barn and felt that he should come over and help us. Afterward I called my folks. I was so excited about talking on a telephone with no wires, in the middle of a barn in the middle of nowhere; I almost forgot my problems.

"My mom answered the phone and instantly began crying as she heard my voice. I assured her I was OK. Between sobs, she cried out, 'Dad, it's our Billy! He's on the phone and he's OK!' Dad took the phone and before anything else could be said, he wanted assurance that I was all right. I thought he was really going to fuss at me for running away as I did, but he didn't say anything; he just wanted assurance I was OK.

"'I'm OK, Dad, really I am! Here Dad, someone here wants to talk to you, his name is Mr. Cecil, and he's kind of like grandpa and has a barn with horses, cows, and a cat, plus a phone with no cord!'

"My dad and Mr. Cecil talked briefly; he assured my dad that I was safe and that he had called the sheriff to come over and help me with the problems that brought me to his barn in the middle of the night.

"'What problems?' I could hear my dad say over the phone as Mr. Cecil had lifted it a little from his ear.

"'I am not sure of all the details, but certainly something made the boy brave a night in the forest and to find shelter in a barn. The sheriff is a personal friend of mine and is personally coming over, I am sure he will be in touch with you soon.' Before he hung up, he gave my dad his phone-with-no-wires phone number so that Dad could stay in touch if he didn't hear back soon.

"He also gave him directions to his barn. It was only a short time before the sheriff came. Mr. Cecil had already asked me to let him talk to the sheriff first, that I was glad to do.

"After about twenty minutes, the sheriff and a deputy came into the barn and sat down on the hay beside me. 'Bill, is that your name?'

"'Yes, sir,' I said with a scared and timid voice.

"'My name is Sheriff Ward, please I am here to help you, so there is no reason to be afraid. I just need to ask you a few questions while we wait for your parents' arrival, we have already called them and they are on their way here now.' The questions Sheriff Wade asked were simple and really were questions about me, not much about what happened, except for names and places.

"My parents arrived in about two hours, we hugged and kissed, and it was sure good to see them. I tried to tell them what happened, but they said, 'Wait.' They just wanted to see me and be with me. That sure made me feel good. In a few minutes, the sheriff came and told my folks they needed to ask me a series of questions, but did not want to do so until they arrived and consented to the questions.

"'Why?' my dad said, 'has he done something wrong?'

"'No, in fact what he has done may have been the bravest thing a young boy his age could have done and could save the lives of many other young boys also,' said the Sheriff.

"'I don't understand,' said Mom.

"'Before you leave, Bill, Mr. Cecil wanted to show you how the telephone setup in his truck works, so you would know for sure what it looked like.'

"'Don't you, Cecil?' said the sheriff as he looked over at him.

"'Sure, I did,' he said, 'would you, folks, mind if I borrow Bill for just a few moments? This is something I know he will really want to see!' My dad seemed to understand why they wanted me to go outside to the truck and agreed to my going. While I was gone, I could see them talking inside, I could hear my mom cry every now and then and when she did, Dad would put his arms around her as if to say, 'it will be all right.'

"After about half an hour, they came out and said, 'Billy, before we go home I think we should go down to the sheriff's office and talk for a while. Will that be all right, son?'

"'Sure, Dad, if that's what you want to do.'

"'Can I ride with you and Mom?'

"The next few hours were spent going over details and providing the information that they knew was difficult for me. There were some questions asked concerning sex, which I have to admit I really was not overly aware of much of it at the time. Sex was something that start giggly parties, as I called it, when the guys who wanted to talk about such things, I was interested in just being a boy; girls had not quite caught up with me yet. However, from the questioning period I had, which was followed up by an investigation, it took little effort for the police investigators to uncover the truth about this man. They learned how he was misleading and using the young boys he was supposed to be teaching and inspiring, and especially as a Sunday school teacher. The teacher had such evidence shown against him, which I later learned, that he plead guilty to multiple charges brought against him and was sentenced to prison for a long time.

"Having done what, I did help many other young boys like me not get taken in by this guy again, and many praised me for having had the courage. But the knowledge of the good that came from it did not erase the fact that this person had violated my trust in him as well as in myself. I was thrust into the knowledge explosion of what type of a man he was and the crimes and sins, which he was committing. He had sexually abused half of the boys in the class.

"My Pastor shared with me from Romans chapter 1 how God views this type of sin of one man with another man, that because of this terrible sin, God had given them up. I tried to understand, but my mind was blocking it. At first I began to blame myself because I felt I had done something wrong, that I was guilty of such ugly things because I was there. I could not forgive him for what he tried to do to me and I left Sunday school with the idea that I would never again ever attend there or church—never.

"'Earth to Mars, Earth to Mars,' I began to hear someone say. As I came to reality, I soon knew it was Mary. 'Are you still with us? You were so deep in thought that I was beginning to feel that you were going to space out on us.' 'Not really,' I replied, 'I was just thinking about some things that happened to me a long time ago, which I feel that it is time to leave it in the past and go on to the future.' Mary wasn't sure what all that meant, but was glad to have me back in communication with her. She talked about what was going to happen that morning and then gave me a second surprise, Sunday school. I had agreed to go to church, but had not realized that to Mary it also meant being early enough for Sunday school. I tried to keep a cool composure, but inside I was having a battle. Mary put her cool, soft hand on my arm, and said in a sweet voice, 'You don't mind coming to my class and sitting with me in Sunday school, do you?' How could anyone, even myself, resist that, so I simply said, 'Nope?' 'Good,' she said, 'turn right at the next street and we are there.'

"The class we attended was the college and career class. There were a good number of single people our age there and the teacher and his wife worked together to lead the class. Mr. Preston was fifty-one, he said, and his wife Judy didn't tell, but must have been close to his age. They were a wonderful couple and really seemed to love what they were doing and each other. It was only a short time before I became comfortable and realized that the only thing I had to fear all these years was fear itself. I was really glad to be there, and to begin to have a burden I had carried for many years begin to lift off my life.

"Following the lesson, we had a question-and-answer period, which I enjoyed and then they thanked each of us for coming, especially the visitors, then Mr. Preston dismissed in prayer. We left the classroom and went to the main church for the service. People were coming from the various classrooms. For the most part, there was a joy in their voices as they spoke to each other. People were friendly, I believe I have never had my hand shaken so much. It was good and made me feel welcomed and almost at home. I did meet a couple of people who I knew during my school days, they were surprised to see me, but delighted.

"Entering the sanctuary was a wonderful experience. It was really beautiful. There were four sections of pews with a wide center aisle. The choir was already in place with about seventy people, and the pianist and organist were softly playing. The color scheme was like a reddish maroon with the carpet and padded pews and seats. The windows were done in an array of colors that blended and gave a spring flower image as you watched the sunbeams filter through the glass. There were four seats for the minister and staff on the platform, the seats were very handsome and appeared to have hand carvings on them. The pulpit looked like it was made of solid cherry wood; it had a beautiful color to it and was very sturdy looking.

"Finding a seat almost halfway down on the second section, we sat down and Mary began speaking first. 'How do you like my church, so far?' 'It's really pretty, I was just admiring the whole layout as we came in,' I said. 'Great,' exclaimed Mary in a cheerful and high voice. 'We have worked hard to make this something that is not only pretty, but also practical and which will honor the Lord as we worship Him here.' 'Well, I am sure it does that,' I replied.

"The choir began to sing such music I do not recall, even from my days of going to church as a young boy. It was simply beautiful, these people needed to make a CD, I thought. They were singing something about an eastern gate and meeting you in the morning, it was a lovely song, but I was not sure what it meant. Everyone quieted down and listened intensely as the choir sang. What an introduction, I was beginning to anticipate what was going to happen next, more singing I hoped. After the choir finished, the director turned and came over to the pulpit. 'Please stand and turn in your songbooks to number 230,' he said. We all stood and began to sing as he led us in this song, and one more.

"The minister, Dr. Tony Baker, came to the platform and led in prayer. After the prayer, he gave the announcements and welcomed the visitors, those visiting for the first time were asked to raise their hand. I didn't raise mine. 'Raise your hand,' said Mary, 'and don't be afraid, they are really interested in knowing who new people like you are.' So I raised my hand. An usher came, gave me a card and a pen. 'Keep the pen,' he said, 'to remind you of your visit with us, please fill out the card and put it in the offering plate when it comes by.' Taking the card, I filled it out in preparation for putting it in the plate.

"The choir sang another song, and then we sang what they called the offertory song. The men passed the plates for the collection; I put in the card and some cash, and then passed the plate down the line. After this, a lady got up and sang a beautiful song as a solo, "Beyond the Sunset," or something like that. I enjoyed it.

"The minister began to speak; he spoke of heaven and what the Lord had prepared for those who had accepted His Son. He also shared what His Son, Jesus Christ, had done on the cross for our sins. I had heard these words before, but had never allowed them to be applied personally to me. I knew that I was not a believer and that I would miss heaven because of my unbelief. I did not want that, someone inside of me was convicting my heart and encouraging me to accept what Christ has done for me. As I listened to the minister speak, my thoughts became focused on my need of salvation. I prayed within myself, 'Lord, I am a sinner and I want to be a Christian, I am not sure how to become one, please show me.' As the minister finished his sermon, and I my prayer, he asked us all to stand. The choir director stood up and said, 'Let's turn to page 276, "Just as I Am." I had heard this song before, but not until now had it had a meaning to me. I realized that God loved me just as I am. He had forgiven me of my sins with the shed blood of His Son on the cross and that I needed to accept Him as my personal Savior. The minister spoke as we sang, 'If there is anyone here who is not a Christian or not sure how to become a Christian, would they please raise their hand, so that I might pray for them.' I was amazed at how quickly I raised my hand, I had not intended to, but the question was exactly what my thoughts were. The minister prayed for those that had raised their hand, and then invited them to come forward in order for someone to take the Bible and show them how they could become a Christian. I was scared and did not want to go forward, more out of pride than anything else. Mary had seen me raise my hand, she slipped her arm around me, and said, 'Bill if you would like to go forward and know about becoming a Christian, I would be willing to go with you.' This was an offer I found difficult to refuse, so we went forward. I did not think this would ever happen to me, but I soon found that love makes a way.

"The minister spoke with me briefly and found out that I was not a Christian, he asked one of the men to take me aside and share with me how I can become a Christian. As I left, I saw Mary kneel at the altar and begin to pray, I was sure she was praying for me. 'Bob Carter is my name,' said the man I had gone with. 'Let me take my Bible and show you a few verses of Scriptures.' He showed me five or six verses, each revealed to me my lost condition and my need of salvation, and he then asked me if I wanted to become a Christian, to which I replied yes! He led me in a prayer in which I asked the Lord to save me and to come into my heart. It was like a heavy burden was lifted from my shoulder. I had no hope, no real joy, and no confidence in the future, but now, I had all that and more. Bob took me back into the church building, they were still singing. As we entered, I noticed my mom and dad were at the altar praying. The minister asked me what had happened to me, I said that I had accepted the Lord as my personal Savior. He shared this with the congregation, who with a loud voice said, 'Amen.' He asked me to stand at the front so the folks could come by and shake my hand, welcoming me into the family of God. My parents had gotten up and were now speaking with him. He shared with the folks that they were my parents and that they had come to get their lives right with the Lord and to join the local church and serve God once again. For you see, they too had stopped going to church on any regular basis after what had happened to me. Mary came and stood by my side as the folks came and greeted me. I was not prepared for this; many hugged my neck like I was a long lost relative that had final come home.

"After the service, the minister spoke with me briefly, he shared with me the Scripture's command for all believers to follow in Scripture baptism, to which I consented to do. If the Lord loved me, like I now knew He did, the least I could do was to do what He wanted me to do. That evening, Mary and I came back to the service and at the close of the service, I was baptized.

"Now the joy that Mary has, and which you have, Jay, became real to me. Mary and I are seriously asking the Lord's direction in our lives. I want to thank you for being faithful to share your faith with me and to have so understood. I have had so much love shown to me, enough to last me for a lifetime. My! What things can happen when love makes a way!" Jay could hardly speak, the joy was so welling up in him that it was all he could do to drive the car. In fact, he pulled over at a safe place and began to share with Bill his joy and his happiness of seeing Bill become a Christian. Jay was surely looking forward to the future of their riding together, they now had so much more in common through Christ. Time was passing on, so Jay started the car and drove to work, that was only a few blocks further down the road. Arriving at the parking lot, Jay asked Bill if he would mind if they had a word of prayer together before they went inside. Bill said, "Sure, but you pray, I'm still not sure about how to do some things." Jay began to pray, "Lord, thank you for Bill's salvation, I ask that you help him each moment of the day, that Satan not try to steal Bill's joy. Help me to be a closer friend and brother that I might share more of you with him, help us both as we work today to put Christ first in everything we do, in Jesus's name I pray, Amen."

"Thanks," said Bill. "I needed that, and guess we had better go inside before we end up being late."

"This is one day I would like to take off," said Jay. "But we can talk more on the way home." With that last thought, they entered the front door and went to their appointed places.

Chapter 3

With the family off to their "appointed places," Nell turned her attention to her place. There was much work for her to do today; first the kitchen needed a complete cleaning and then the rest of the house. This was not a chore for her to do; it was a service for which she felt the Lord wanted her to do for Him and for her family, whom she loved dearly. Before she began her daily routine, Nell had become accustomed to just sitting and relaxing for a while, over that extra cup of coffee and usually the last piece of toast. This morning was no exception, she loved to sit by the picture window in the dining room, and this allowed her to see the backyard and the woods beyond. What a wonderful place she expressed out loud as if talking with someone. *The Lord surely has blessed us, for which we are thankful.* She was still amazed at how inexpensive they were able to get the lovely large two-story home at the edge of the city, and she knew the Lord was in it. When they first moved in, the place was a wreck, the house needed major remodeling, and the entire yards had to be completely landscaped. That was ten years ago, for the past ten years they had worked hard to make their house a home. With all the major work done, she was going to enjoy all that the Lord had blessed her with.

Looking over the grounds, she saw several deer feeding at the far right corner of the property. It was a common sight to see the deer, they came often and Nell felt assured they felt they were safe. Most of the time, the deer would bolt away if they went into their part of the yard. However, there were times in which the deer lingered to see if they were coming to them or just doing something away from them and not being a threat to them. This morning, there were three does and a fawn. She thought she saw a buck a short distance in the cover of the woods, but was not sure. *The bucks usually did not come out of cover, perhaps they just did not trust man, and I must admit rightfully so.*

Over toward the left of the property, there were several rabbits feeding on the grass. *With the heavy dew, they were getting their water and feed at the same time*, thought Nell. There were several fruit-bearing trees planted in the area. "I wish we had some citrus trees, however we are too far north for them to survive," said Nell out loud as if she was talking with someone. They had planted several cherry and apple trees and one plum tree. Each of the trees gave a good crop last year, and she was hoping for one this year. They ate the fresh fruit as long as it would last and canned the balance. The canned fruit they shared with their pastor and visiting missionaries throughout the year.

As Nell enjoyed the view, she knew that while it would be pleasant to sit there all day, there were her appointed things to do in her appointed place, and she needed to get busy doing it. *Strange*, she thought, *how Billy prayed such a prayer, he must have learned the word appointed in school and was now using it*. It was appropriate and even made explanation easy, especially to Patrick Henry, who understood it when she explained the word at the breakfast table. With a quick prayer, thanking the Lord for her salvation, her family, and her home, Nell went about her work. She began in the kitchen, dishes and pots and pans. It seemed like a lot, but Nell had a system which made the work go quickly, of course the automatic dishwasher too most of the hard work out of the task. In fact, she finished the kitchen so quickly she said, speaking to that imagination of hers, "If I keep this pace up I can have time to run the errands I've been wanting to do, so I guess I'll just go for it." She began upstairs, and before she realized she had gone through the entire house. Her family was generally a neat family, and therefore her work was more of tidying or putting things back into place. They had wisely chosen to restore the hardwood floors in all rooms of the house, with exception of the den. This saved her many hours of work to vacuum. They had taken the one large bedroom that was downstairs and made it into a den.

This room had a deep carpet and a cozy atmosphere. This was where she came to relax often and where most of the family came to play games or to be together. There was a good-sized television, but they watched little of it. There was so little worth watching that as a family Jay had gotten all of them to agree to a standard of moral decency before they turn the television on. Jay was a wonderful husband and a good father to the children. He usually took a stand on things, which he felt were right and scriptural for leadership in their house and family. Nell loved him for this and supported him 100 percent in his effort. He was trying to put Christ first in his home without being legalistic, performing the spirit of the law versus the letter of the law, as he said it. Having completed her tasks, she sat in her favorite chair in the den. She was taking these few extra minutes to think of the things which she wanted to do today. She also wanted to complete her own private devotions.

Nell liked the quietness of the morning and usually found time to stop in the den and do her daily Bible readings and prayers. She had read her verses; she chose to read one chapter from the book of Proverbs each day. Since today was the twenty-third, it was the chapter she would read. Her Sunday school teacher had challenged her class to do this, and Nell took the challenge. She found it enjoyable and had done it each month for the entire year. She also read some passages in 1 Peter; this is where her private study of the Word of God had taken her. She enjoyed reading and studying it verse by verse. She would cross-reference thoughts and verses to try to get a full meaning of each verse. She had learned many years ago that the best way to learn was to teach. She had previously taught a class and had not gotten out of the habit of studying as if she was going to teach a lesson on the text. When she was alone in the house, Nell often spoke out loud, instead of just in her thoughts. She said to herself, *Well, if I think it inside then there is no difference if I say it outside, besides by saying my thoughts it helps me to be clearer on the direction I feel the Lord would have me to take.* As she finished her Bible study and prayer time, she left the den to go to her room and prepare to go a few places. She usually put on a simple, easy dress for the mornings, and unless she had an early appointment or guests, she waited for the family to be off before she did the extra things a lady would do to fix herself up before she went out in public. As she walked to her room, she began to speak to herself, *Nell, you study as if you are preparing to teach and you have done that for years, should you be teaching? Is there a need for more teachers down at the church?* During her devotion time, she had thought about why she studied the way she did. It was during those thoughts that the Holy Spirit had pricked her heart with conviction about her not teaching now. She had stopped due to some illness which took her several months to get over, but that was in the past, when was she going to get into the future. "Jay and I have talked about this," she said, "and he had encouraged me to start again, for he knew I loved to teach and enjoy the children so much." This morning the conviction was really heavy on her heart and in speaking to herself, she said, "All right, Lord, I'll do it! I was going by the church this morning to drop off some canned fruit for the visiting missionary, and if the pastor is there I will speak with him, perhaps there is an opening somewhere. I guess I like the fifth grade best, but I want to be flexible and teach where the Lord leads my pastor to ask me to teach."

"Too much thinking," said Nell as she walked into her room. "Now I've gotten myself committed to doing something for the Lord again, well, that's not too bad, the Lord wants the help, that's why He uses us, and I need the opportunity. It helps me give my abilities and talents to others for the Lord's honor and glory. Well, if I am to meet with the pastor and talk, I guess I had better dress a little different than I had originally planned." What Nell had planned was OK, she was just dropping things off and going to the store and to visit some people she already visited on a regular basis to share things of the Lord with. However, in respect to the pastor, she felt she should look better. *He would not mind, but I would have,* thought more of Nell. Nell was always careful about her dress; she wanted to be known for being a modest Christian woman who loved the Lord. She had learned early in her marriage that her dress had much to do with how people perceived her. When she first got married, she wanted to dress attractive and somewhat provocative for her husband; she loved him and wanted to excite him about her. He was her husband, and if she did things to attract him and make him desire her, she felt it was right. They were married, and God had given them to each other to enjoy, including sex. *It must have worked,* she thought, as she had three children. However, the lesson she learned was that, if she was trying to dress to attract Jay, she had to be careful what she wore and where she wore it. For while it may attract Jay, it also attracted other men! She had gotten several men flirting with her, which she admitted she liked the attention and appreciated the fact that she was still accepted as a lovely woman. However, when one man went beyond being friendly to being fresh and forward, it brought her to reality that it was not right. When the man made a pass at her and she rejected him, he got upset and said to her, "You dress to tease, yet you are not willing to please, so what kind of woman are you?" With that comment made, Nell left the office she was at and quickly came back to her home. She cried all the way. She had almost allowed flirtation and the like of it to ruin the best things in her life. Her most prized treasures were her relationship to her Lord and to her husband.

After she arrived home, she had gone into the den and cried, thankful that no one else was there. She prayed and asked the Lord to forgive her sin. She had started by teasing her husband, but secretly down inside she had also enjoyed the attraction of other men, not that she wanted them, but because she wanted to be accepted as a beautiful and desirable woman; pride was the real sin here. Having made her confession with the Lord and having felt the reassurance of His forgiveness, she had vowed that all that she did to attract a man in the future would be in her home to her husband. When she went out in public, it would be to be an example of a Godly woman. Having settled these thoughts in her mind, she prepared herself and dressed for the day.

It was almost eleven when she left the house. *The day is half gone,* she thought, *I must hurry if I am to accomplish all I need to do and still get back in time to prepare supper. Where do I go first? I had promised Sally I would come to her house for lunch. And I need to go by the church and the store. If I go to the church first and speak with the pastor, it may take too long, so I will go to Sally's first. Sally had said just pop in, and we would fix something for lunch. Then I'll go see the*

Pastor, drop off the stuff for the missionaries, and then to the store. That should get me back home around three, enough time to be there before the children arrive and time enough to start supper. Driving away from the house, she headed to Sally's home.

Sally was a widow and a single mother who was new to their church. After she had visited, the pastor asked if she would call on her. Having met her, I found her to be a sweet girl who had had many difficulties in life and just needed a good Christian friend, which I hoped to be to her. Sally did not live far from her and therefore she arrived almost before she had finished the thought-planning for the day. As she knocked on the door, she hears Sally call out, "Come on in, it's open." Sally was expecting Nell and had unlocked the door just a few minutes before she arrived. Sally had a nice two-bedroom home, modest and affordable to her on her limited income. Nell had visited twice before, each time being friendly and allowing Sally time to know for sure that she just wanted to be her friend. The place was completely different than when she last saw it. Someone had really fixed up the outside, and it looked like a range house with rustic barn-type fence and yard decorations, even cactus. Did Sally come into some money or find a rich friend? She was sure the fellow who sold it to her had not done it; he just wasn't the type. He had sold it to her in need of many repairs, and that was really the only reason that Sally was able to purchase the home. Nell thought to herself as she entered the house that someone must surely be on Sally's side.

Sally had called out from the kitchen, "Come on back, I've started lunch." As Nell walked down the hallway, she noticed that Sally had been working on the place since her last visit. The hallway had been repainted, and the decorations were very pretty and tasteful. They gave a western flavor to the house. *She must be from out west somewhere*, thought Nell. As Nell entered the kitchen, she could smell the food, but was not sure what it was. "What's for lunch?" Nell asked. "How about homemade chicken soup with lots of rice and spice and a salad on the side, iced tea if you want it or I can make coffee," replied Sally. "Everything sounds fine to me, I'll stay with the tea, already had my second cup of coffee today and that's my limit," replied Nell. The kitchen looked very nice, it was small but well-organized. One of the things Nell liked best was that the appliances, including the stove and refrigerator, were centrally located so that one could stand at the stove, reach into the refrigerator on one side and the work counter on the other side, without having to walk back and forth. *The kitchen had been painted also, and she had decorated it to look like a country cook's house,* thought Nell. "Wow, does this place ever look nice, Sally, you have really been busy at work since the last time I was here, how did you ever do all this by yourself?" asked Nell. "I didn't," said Sally. "Let me tell you what happened."

"First, let me say how much I appreciate your coming to visit me, it has really meant a lot to me, and I do count you as a friend, if that's all right?"

"Sure," replied Nell, "I was hoping to be accepted as a friend, for that is what I would like to be."

"Well, consider yourself accepted. You are my number one, first friend here."

"Sounds great to me," said Nell. "Now please tell me about who helped you fix the place up. It really looked drab when I was here before, and of course, I didn't say anything, for I knew you were doing your best and had done the best you could have under your circumstances. Now tell me what happened."

"As you are aware, I have visited your church several times, I really like the people, and the pastor and his wife are very lovely people. I have not known such friendliness and kindness. In fact, I really did not believe it existed before this. You're Pastor and his wife visited, then you visited, and after your last visit, one of the deacons and his wife visited, Ted and Sue Belfast."

"Yes, I know them, they really do love the Lord and have a burden for people," said Nell.

Sally continued sharing, "They visited to get to know me and thank me for visiting the church, they did not try to pry into my life and what brought me here or my circumstances of being a single mother, for which I was thankful. They were interested in me as a person, my visiting their church, and what needs I might have. Ted spoke of spiritual things and did ask me a few questions, for which I gave him the best answers I knew. Sue seemed interested in my having just moved in and perhaps could use some help in getting my place set up. She asked, 'What could I do to help you, dear? With a little help, we could really fix this place up to your liking.' I answered, 'I've spoken to the man I bought it from and he said he sells his places as is, if I wanted to fix things or upgrade things it was OK with him, but I would have to do it at my expense. If he did it, he would have to raise the sale price for the property. I thanked him, but said I prefer he leave it as it is, for I could only afford the house payment I have now and did not want to have to pay more.'

"Sue thanked me for my being honest with her and said, 'Dear, would you mind if some of the ladies at the church and I help you fix your place up?' Ted also spoke up and said, 'I could get a few men to help do the heavy work also.' 'I could hardly keep from crying,' said Sally. I just did not know what to think of people like this, what possible motive could they have to want to do this, there was nothing in it for them that I could think of, and do people really do things like this for others. How could so much love find a way to my home? I had shared with them that I had lost my husband and was a widow. Ted replied, 'Well. as a deacon of the church one of my responsibilities is to see our church minister to the widows and orphans, and we need to see how we can help you.'"

"Thank you, Lord," said Nell out loud, "for a deacon and his wife who both saw their ministry and also performed it, tell me more," Nell said to Sally in the same breath.

"Last week, I received a call from Sue, she wanted to know if it would be all right for several ladies of the church to come and spend the day with me to help fix things up around the house. She explained they had gotten paint and some decorations to make the place look nice. I had told her I was from Texas, and I had always wanted to do my place over in a western style. 'Sure,' I said. 'Should I fix lunch?' 'No,' Sue replied, 'we don't want to be a burden to you, just a blessing, so we have a large picnic planned and even a table and chairs so we can set under the shade tree and have a nice lunch, if that is all right.' 'I would love it,' I told her and invited them to come over.

"Last Tuesday, they were here at eight in the morning, they had work clothes on and all sorts of paints, rollers, brushes, wallpaper, and boxes of other stuff. Sue was the first to speak. She introduced the crew. I thanked them all for coming, I was not sure how or what they were going to do, I was thankful for the help and felt I should just let them do what was best. I had a two-year-old to care for and was carrying my second child, which I hoped to be a girl, so I could not do a lot to help. 'Sue,' I said, 'I am not sure what all you can do and as you can see I can be of little help. I thank you for coming, and I trust that whatever you do, or how you do it, that it will just look fine.' 'We got together as the deacon's wives and a few other ladies of the church where we discussed your need and your desire for a western theme. If it's OK with you, we do have a plan that I can show you, if you approve them we will go to work,' said Sue. 'Go to work and let me see the plan after it's done, I can understand it better from seeing what you have done than reading the plan.' 'Great,' said Sue, 'we don't think you will be disappointed. By the way, two of our deacons work second shift and will be coming over this morning to do some of the outside work, is that OK?' 'Sure,' I said.

"Before they began to work, Sue asked if we could have a word of prayer, asking the Lord to bless our efforts today. I was not accustomed to doing such things, but said, 'Please go ahead.' Sue prayed briefly asking the Lord to give them wisdom for what needed to be done and success for their efforts. After the prayer, they began to work all over the place, at what seemed to be at the same time. It was evident they had a plan, for each thing they did made sense to the next thing they did. We had met in the living room, and that is where they started first, in a short time they had cleared the furniture away from the walls, cleaned the walls, and had started to paint a beautiful beige color. Being eight months pregnant, I was getting sick from the smell of the paint. Sue noticed this and said, 'Sally, I believe the paint might make you feel ill, why don't you sit on the porch and have a nice glass of lemonade while we ladies kick up the dust and make a mess in here.' 'Sounds good to me,' I said. I shared that I was getting sick and appreciated her noticing it. Sue walked me out to the porch, gave me a glass of lemonade, and made sure I was comfortable. Just as she did, the men arrived. Sue introduced them as Pat and Mike. I said, 'Thank you for coming I really don't know how to thank you people or even what to say, this is like a dream and I am afraid to pinch myself for I might wake up and find it is.' 'It's no dream,' said Pat, 'at our church, our pastor has faithfully taught us over the years that we have a responsibility to care for people, especially you're being a widow, and when the opportunity came up, we knew that love will find a way for us to help you.' 'Well, thanks for coming, do you have a plan also?' 'Ted had told us at our weekly deacon's prayer meeting what your needs were. He said that you liked a western theme. We have some ideas to discuss with you to see if you would like them.' 'I like them already, so just go ahead and do what you think is best, that will make your job easier and leave it as a surprise to me as to what it is. I almost feel like leaving home and coming back to find it heaven.' 'Thanks for the confidence,' said Pat, 'we think you will be happy with what we have planned.' And with that, he and Mike unloaded their truck, had a word of prayer together, and started working.

"'Sally,' said Sue, 'you make me just think of a lovely idea, there is a lot going on over here today and the smell, and noise, and dust are not good for you. Would you mind going and visiting with Jennie, the single mother you met at Sunday school. If you visited with her, that would give you a chance to make a new friend and also get you out of this mess.' 'Would Jennie mind?' I asked. 'No,' Sue said, 'I had told her at church that if the paint smell bothered you that I might ask you to come over, so therefore she would be expecting you, in fact I am supposed to call if you don't come.' 'Well, I guess I had better go,' I told her. It took me a few minutes to get ready and then I drove over to Jenny's house, she only lived a few blocks from me, I had lunch with her one Sunday after church, and she was a nice person. Just before I left, Sue had said she would call when it was time for me to come home. When I arrived at Jenny's, I was warmly received, I just sat and relaxed. I believe I needed that restful day as much as I needed the house fixed up. Jenny had insisted that I just sit and relax; she waited on me all day and cared for my little boy as if he were her own. While I was there, we talked about many things. Nell, I wanted to share about the house having been fixed up with you, but I knew you would see that for yourself when you arrived. I am really thankful for what they did, but first let me tell you what happened at

Jenny's; one thing we talked about was God and who Jesus was. I had a difficult childhood, an abusive dad and then an abusive husband. I thought I deserved all that because I was someone that really did not deserve to be loved. My dad had done things to me that I would never forget or get over for the rest of my life and I hated my mom because she knew what he was doing and did nothing to stop it. My husband abused me. I could take the beatings and cussing out most of the time, but what the bottom of the barrel was one night he and his buddies were over having a drinking poker game. My husband was losing pretty heavy and had given this one guy several markers worth about 300 dollars. I was attractive and had a pretty good figure, this guy had stared at me every time I came into the room that night, and it was clear what he was thinking about. After the game, the other guys had left except for this one guy. I heard him say to my husband, 'Well, it's payday, pal. You owe me a lot of money and I need it, so pay up.' 'I don't have that kind of money with me, but I can give it to you on payday.' 'That's not the way it works, but tell you what I do, you get your pretty little wife to come in here and agree to a wager and I will play you a high stakes hand, your debt against the night in bed with your wife.' I thought my husband would fly into a rage and throw this bum out, but he didn't, he gave excuses and said he didn't think he could talk me into it. I was crushed; he was willing to give me to this guy if he could talk me into it. I was not a wife; I was only his property. I guess that guy heated it up for him. He finally came into the kitchen. 'Honey,' he said, 'I need to talk to you about something.' 'I know,' I said, 'I heard the whole thing. Do you really want me to sleep with this guy?' 'Well, I owe him a lot of money and I am sure that he is going to hurt me, maybe our house and maybe you if he does not get his way, besides he put it as high stakes for a card draw. I was really winning when the game finished, and I think I can take this guy.' I was completely demoralized. I did not know how much worse things could get. I thought maybe this is why my dad did what he did to me. I was evil because I attracted men this way. I refuse to speak my husband's name, even in telling about him so I said, 'Listen, if this is what you want me to do, then I will do it. I hate it and I hate you, from this time on, we may be a couple but we are not married.' 'Honey, you wait and see, I'll win and it'll all be over with, and I'll never do this again.' I had to go into the room with him. This guy wanted to hear me say that I agreed, that I would not fight him, and that I would do whatever he wanted. I said, 'As long as it doesn't hurt me.' I wish I had not agreed, for I had no idea what his "whatever" meant. But I found out, they each drew a card and he won. 'Your place or mine, honey?' he said. 'I care less, I may do this, you may use me, but I will just be there, that's all.' That's been the worst night of my life. After that, I did not care what happened to me or if I lived. It was only because I was carrying my child, I had just found out I was pregnant and had not even told my husband yet. Afterward, I took what seemed like a thousand baths, but could not wash away the disgust and shame that I felt. I hated my husband and wished him dead. I could have killed him myself, but since I did not have the courage to protect myself, how could I do that to someone else? After he came home the next day, we said little, he didn't ask any questions and tried to be nice. I didn't want his being nice. For the next month, we hardly spoke and I would not let him touch me. One day, a policeman came to my house, he asked who I was and for identification. After he was sure of who I was, he said that my husband had left a bar a few hours ago, he was really drunk and had caused an accident with fatal injuries to several people, including himself. I was asked to come and identify the body, I did not want to, however I went to get the matter over with. There was some insurance, enough for me to settle our affairs and move here, and some to keep me going until the benefits from his work and social security became available. That is what we live off of now. After this child is born, I plan to get some training and find a job.

"Life was over for me, as far as I was concerned. I only lived for my children; I wanted to show them love in the right ways that I never found love. That was until I met you, folks. Jenny listened to me, she didn't try to condemn me, and in fact she was very understanding. I had expressed that there was no one that I had known before coming there that had ever loved me or cared for me. With a tender smile, Jenny replied, 'I know one man that did.' 'How could you? You did not even know me until I came here.' 'No, I didn't, but

He did. You see, Sally, His name is Jesus, He loves you just as you are, He accepts you just as you are. He loved you so much that He gave His life on a cross for you. He gave His life that you might live and have joy and peace. Would you like for me to take my Bible and show you more?' 'Yes,' I said. She showed me a lot of verses and explained what things meant. I began to have some hope. 'Before, I could not and would not have listened to anyone, except I could not disbelieve the kindness which so many of you, from your church have shown me since I've been here.' Because of that, I was willing to listen with an open heart and mind. 'Sally, I accepted Jesus Christ as my personal Savior. I know now that He had forgiven all my sins and took care of them on the cross. I have even prayed for those that abused me. My prayer was that one day they might come to know Jesus also. That love would find a way in their hearts as it had in mine.'"

We both cried and laughed together, I was so happy. I knew the folks at the church had done something to help her, but I did not realize that all this had been done. They had shared briefly what they were doing, but wanting God to get the glory, they just said this was an opportunity to serve the Lord. Just think, I had prayed and came planning on talking to Sally about the Lord today, and here she is blessing me with her testimony. What a day, how wonderful it is when love finds a way, thought Nell.

After a few minutes of Sally and Nell crying and praising the Lord together for what had happened, Nell finally spoke. "Sally, this is wonderful and not only can we be friends, we are now sisters in the Lord. And as my sister, I want to be the first to help you as you begin your spiritual pathway. In Matthew chapter 28, verses 19 to 20, we are told to disciple those that believe. If you would allow me, I would like to meet with you each week and talk about the Bible and help you to begin your new Christian life, would you like for me to do that?"

"I sure would, at least up until I have to go into the hospital for the baby," said Sally.

"How about this," added Nell, "I'll come over here each week and meet with you. We will have a Bible study together for perhaps an hour. When it's close to the time for the baby to be born, I will come more often or ask one of the ladies to come and stay with you. Remember that you are not in this thing alone. How does that sound?"

"Great," said Sally. "I was worried that the baby might start coming and I am alone here with my boy."

"Just thought of something, when it's time for your baby, why not have your little boy, John, stay with us? We have a spare bedroom, and between my three children he will get lots of attention, I guarantee it," said Nell.

"Would you really do that for me? I don't understand all of you people and I don't understand why you are so willing to give and not expect anything in return," Sally said between sobs as she began to cry.

"The difference is easy to say, sometimes hard to really comprehend, you see when you have Christ as your Savior and you then find that when others have a need, then love finds a way. We love you because Christ first loved us. What we do for you we do for the Lord, for He said when you have done for the least of the saints, you have done it unto Him. Our pastor is a kind, loving person. He has taught us to know and appreciate the love of Christ, and he has also taught us to share that love with others. That is why when our deacons saw your need, they responded, and so did their wives. As I express your need for company during your last days of waiting for delivery, there will be no problem getting ladies to volunteer to come and be with you, in fact we may have to turn some away. Our folks are like that, I have found in Christ. And in this local church is a true love both expressed and demonstrated. As a Christian, when you come to the place in life that you turn all over to Him and you stand ready to serve, you will find He will and He can use you. Each day and in every thing, I ask, 'Is this what the Lord would have me do, or say, or go?' As the Spirit of the Lord gives me confidence, then I do, or say, or go. God does lead in the small things in our lives, as well as in the major decisions.

"This sounds too much like I am a teacher, which reminds me that in my morning devotions I had noticed that my Bible study was structured as if I were preparing to teach, I used to teach Sunday school classes. The Lord convicted me for not returning to teaching after an illness I had, and I had just this morning committed to Him that I would teach again. In fact, after I leave here my next stop was to go by the church and share with the pastor that I was available to teach where needed the most."

"It sounds like the Lord has confirmed that decision here with me today as you have taught me much in such a short time," said Sally. "This is so much. I never knew such love could exist. I guess the real tragedy of my life is that until now I have never known what love really was, but I am so happy I have found it here, in Christ and in my new friends, or should I say family."

"Both," Nell replied, "for we are your family and we are your friends."

"Well, sister, what should I do next? How do I become a helping member of the family? I want to give, not just get," said Sally with a new happiness in her voice.

"May I offer a plan that will help you as a new Christian, and if I can, then please get a pencil and paper to write it down, I find that helps me," said Nell.

Sally left for a few moments to find the paper and pencil. This gave Nell a short time to collect her thoughts and to offer a quick prayer for wisdom and confidence as she helped her new sister. *Isn't it wonderful how the Lord uses us if we are just available?* thought Nell.

"I found them," explained Sally as she returned to the room.

"Then get ready to write, and I will try to give them to you in some sort of priority order. If I missed, we can correct it later. What I would like to ask you to do is some study on your own and some follow-up work that I think might be helpful to you. I've given some serious thought and prayer to this, in just this short time, and I hope you have confidence that I want to help you as well as love you in Christ," said Nell.

"Sure, I know you have my best interest at heart and only want what's best for me. I am convinced of that. If I don't understand something nor why, would you explain it more to me?" replied Sally.

"Always, ask anything you like, it is best that you understand as much as possible. There are things in God's Word I do not fully understand, so I know I have to accept some things by faith. Even accepting those things by faith I have confidence that God said what he meant and meant what He said, so it will be all right, even if I don't fully understand it," said Nell.

"OK, I'm ready to write, list away," said Sally with a happy spark in her voice.

"Here we go," replied Nell. "First, read the Gospel of John, that's the fourth book of the New Testament as follows: (a) The first time, read it like you would a regular book, don't stop to understand it or comprehend it, read it just like you were reading an essay; (b) The second time, read it a little bit slower and try to focus on the picture of what the book is giving. (c) The third time, read it and begin to stop and find blessings in the parts you seem to understand and make a note of the parts you do not understand. (d) The fourth time, read it and try to understand more about each chapter as you can. Ask yourself these questions: What do I find as a promise in this chapter? What do I find as a command in this chapter? What does this chapter tell me about Jesus? And what does this chapter challenge me to do in my life as a Christian?

"Second, each day make yourself a list of people or things you feel you should pray for or about. Then each day, pray over that list. Prayer is simply your speaking to God about what is in your heart and your seeking His help in the needs of the people you list or the things you need, asking that His will be done in both.

"Third, our pastor, as I am assured you are already aware, is really one of the finest men of God that I have ever known. He is like us, he is not perfect, but then, who is? He tries to do the best and be the truest example before us as he can, in my book I gave him an A+. One thing you may not know about him is that he is an excellent counselor, well-trained, and has helped so many of our church members and their friends. I could give you endless testimonies of how the Lord has used him to help others. I am saying this for a reason. Sally, over the past years, going back to your childhood, you have been taken advantages of and abused. In many cases, you blamed yourself for being evil or that kind of person as you told me. I feel that if you would go to pastor for some counseling sessions in which he would, using the Word of God help you overcome some of the hidden emotions of the past. Right now you are feeling great because of all that has happened to you in the last couple of months, but what happens when you have a few days to sit and remember the past? This one thing I recommend almost above all else.

"Fourth, as a new Christian, you would want to be faithful to what the Word of God has for you. One of the first things the Bible has a new believer to do is to follow the Lord in believer's baptism. Baptism is not needed for salvation; it is done to show others that you have been saved. What happens is this, you go forward in the church service during the invitation time, tell the pastor that you have come to confess that you have accepted Christ as your personal Savior and want to be obedient to His command to be baptized. They may baptize you right then, so be sure to have a change of clothes handy. They may schedule you later if you wish. When you are baptized, you and the pastor, or his assistant pastor, will go into the baptistery with you. He may ask you to reconfirm your faith in Christ, and after having done so, he will cover your nose and put you under the water and bring you back up. It only takes two to three seconds under the water and he won't drop you, so nothing to be afraid of. Baptism symbolizes several things: (1) it's a testimony before all present that you had already accepted Christ and now make it publicly known; (2) as you are put under the water, it shows being buried in the likeness of His (Christ's) death; And (3), as you are brought up out of the water in the likeness of His resurrection.

"Fifth, In our church there are several ways to become a member. First, by acceptance of a letter from a church of like faith and your confirmation you have already had scriptural baptism as I explained above. Second, by statement of faith that you have had scriptural baptism and that you are in agreement with the statement of faith as presented, this is usually the case when someone asks for membership, but their former church has closed or you cannot find their address. Third, by being baptized. If you follow through and be baptized then you will automatically become a member, just like me.

"Now your questions?" said Nell.

Sally began with, "Do I have to go for counseling and what kind of questions is he going to ask me?"

"As a trained counselor, he would only ask you the questions that are proper to help you, as for going, the better question is, 'Does Sally need this help?' That's your question to answer."

"In my heart, I really need help. I know that, but I am not sure I can overcome my fear of not wanting to go."

Nell replied, "If I set it up for you with the pastor, take you to the first session or two, would that make it any easier?"

"Yes, it would," replied Sally.

"Then I'll do it. After I leave here today, I am going by the church and can set it then, will that be OK?"

"This must be one of those 'accepting by faith things you spoke of,'" said Sally. "I trust you, and therefore if you feel strongly he can help me, then I will follow your advice. You have been kind and gracious to me in all other things, and I feel you have my best interest at heart. Yes, I will go if you set it up. Will you also go with me at the end of the service to tell the pastor that I want to be faithful to the Lord by being baptized?"

"It would be my honor," replied Sally.

It had been such a wonderful experience that Nell had lost all track of time and found that she barely had enough time to go to the church and get home before her children did. She explained this to Sally who understood. After a hug and a prayer with Sally, she left for the church. If she did not make it on time, the events she just witnessed was worth it, the other parts she could do tomorrow. However, she got to the church rather quickly. It seemed the Lord knew her situation, and every streetlight was green for her, she did not have to stop one time, which has never happened before, she thought as she drove into the church parking lot. She was happy to see both the pastor's and missionaries' cars still there.

Parking as close to the church office door as she could, because she had to leave the canned fruit she brought, she almost raced getting out of her car and into the church office. She came in so quickly that she almost knocked the pastor down; he had just come out of his office for a cold soda out of the breakroom when Nell flew inside.

"Sorry," said Nell. "I was running late, and for a good reason which I need to share with you right away, and also I have some more canned fruit for you and the missionaries in my car."

"Well, let's see how we can do this and help you gain your lost time." Several of the young boys of the church were sitting in the breakroom having a soda, so the pastor leaned into the room and said, "Boys, would you mind getting the boxes of canned fruit out of Nell's car and bring them in here, putting them on the table?"

"Yes, sir," said the boys in unison. "We'll do it right away." And they left out almost as fast as Nell had come in. "You may be starting a new trend in fast service around here," said the pastor to Nell as he asked her to step into his office. As they entered, Nell noticed that the missionary was sitting in his office, where they must have been discussing whatever. "Oh, I did not mean to break up your meeting. I can wait outside for a few minutes if you need me to," said Nell. Pastor answered, "I know you have to get home to be there when your children come, what's on your mind or do you need to speak to me in private?"

"Well," Nell hesitated to say more, but then knew this was Missionary Robert Howard. He was a Godly man and would probably understand what she had to say and would make a good prayer warrior for Sally, then she continued, "No, please stay, what I have to say, in part is private, but I feel you would keep the confidence that is needed. Pastor," she continued, "I just spent two hours with Sally. She is the girl you asked me to visit, and I have some wonderful news. The other day while she was at Jennie's house, she accepted Christ as her personal Savior."

"I know," said the Pastor. "Sue found out about it when she called to tell Sally she could come home when they were finished decorating. But tell me more."

"Being a new Christian, I knew she needed follow-up, so I offered to come over once a week to have a Bible study with her and to help her with her little boy, John, when the baby's due. I also gave her some Scripture to read and two more things." Running out breath, she paused for a moment.

"Take your time," Pastor said, "I have a feeling the next two things are going to be exciting, and if you don't catch your breath, you may lose too much of it." Having regained her control, she slowly gave them the other two things. "First, Sally has agreed to come forward for baptism in the next service if I will come forward with her. And second, she has had a really rough life, terrible abuse. She went from an abusive father to an abusive husband who was killed in a car wreck he caused as a drunk driver. That's why she is a widow. I suggested that she come to you for a few counseling sessions, and she agreed if I would set it up with you for her, could she come?"

"Sure she can," replied the pastor. "Just get my secretary to schedule her at my next earliest appointment. With her near delivery, I feel we should meet as early as possible. It would help her if you come forward with her this Sunday morning, ask her to come prepared and we will baptize her then, if she feels right about it in her condition, I don't think it makes a difference, but it's her choice. Is there anything else?" asked the Pastor.

"Yes, one more thing I almost forgot, with her nearing full term, she is alone in her house with that two-year-old boy, could we ask some ladies of the church to volunteer to sit with her? I will go once or twice a week for a Bible study, perhaps if any other ladies go, they can have a Bible study with her, I could make up the lessons so we had a pattern to help disciple her properly," said Nell.

"Sounds like a good plan to me, do you have time to be in charge of this project? If you do, then I will make the announcements and just ask the ladies to schedule with you," said the pastor.

"Sure, just ask them to call me. Now one more thing," said Nell, "I almost forgot. The first reason I was coming to see you and Brother Robert about was the canned fruit which is now in the breakroom. Take all you want and if any is left, just put in the Mission's pantry. Also in my devotions this morning, I noticed that I still used the pattern of always study as if I am teaching. I always get more from my lessons if I study as if I was going to teach. As I did this, the Holy Spirit touched my heart with this question, 'Nell, why aren't you teaching?' I know I stopped some time ago because of that serious illness and surgery I had, but I feel that I need to be back on the job of being available to teach. Pastor," Nell asked, "I feel the Lord wants me to begin teaching again, I would love to teach firth grade girls if there is a need, but I also promised the Lord I would make myself available and trust Him to show you where I could be used best."

"Nell, you are such a blessing," said Pastor. "I wish more people would listen to the leadership of the Lord in their lives like this, we have many needs for teachers and workers, and few has come forth because the Lord really convicted them to do so. Too many want to be prodded, and that's not my style. I do have several ideas of areas where someone like you could make a serious impact on the lives of others, but it would take me time to share them with you. Would it be best for you to come back tomorrow when we would have time to discuss them in detail?"

"That would be best," replied Nell. "I really need to leave now if I were going to be home when the children arrive home from school."

"Fine," said the pastor as he shook her hand and thanked her for the fruit and all the good news. Robert, the missionary, spoke, "Nell, thanks for the fruit and the refreshing testimony. By how God can use someone who is willing to be used, perhaps you and Jay can visit our mission field someday. I have to warn you, I would certainly be praying for the Lord to leave you both there helping us."

"Thanks," said Nell. "I appreciate the confidence and thought, but I'm not sure about the visit, must run, goodbye." As she said those words, she almost leaped out the door and into her car. Driving onto the street, she said to herself, *Nell, slow down, you have enough time to make it safely, forget the store and go straight home and you will make it, OK? Just plan something else for dinner.* Listening to herself, she said, *I agree* and headed home. She arrived before anyone else, so she quickly went upstairs to change to more comfortable clothes and then dashed into the kitchen to reinvent her supper plans.

Chapter 4

Billy was the first to arrive at the bus, followed by Patrick Henry, and then June. He usually jumped on the bus and hoped the rest made it, however, this morning it was different. He waited until Patrick Henry was aboard and then he followed June onto the bus. Mom had observed this from the front steps. *Is my son learning manners and respect? I hope so.* Billy did have a purpose in letting them on the bus first. For the past several days, a few of the boys had been picking on his sister, they could not do that and get away with it. June was his sister, and if she needed to be picked on, then he could handle that. He sometimes hated how he treated her personally, especially in public when peer pressure was at its greatest. He really did love her. However, he had determined that others may mess with him, but they "better not mess" with his June or his Patrick Henry.

As he climbed on the bus and started down the aisle, he found that his plan had worked. Two boys had stopped June and were poking at her and messing up her hair. They were so intent in what they were doing that they did not see Billy until he was upon them. Billy was large for his age and was a strong boy. He grabbed both boys at the same time, pulled them out of their seats, and forced them to the back of the bus. He really wanted to hit them, but he controlled his temper. Setting them down, he said, loud enough for all on the bus to hear, "That's my sister you are messing with, and if I ever catch you touching her again, you will answer to me, and that goes for my brother Patrick Henry also." Staring directly into their eyes, with a strong determined stare that began to put fear into them, he repeated himself. "Do you, kids, understand what I am saying?"

"Yes," they both repeated. "We were just having a little fun, we were not going to hurt her." Billy pulled their hair and poked them both. "Did that feel like fun to you?" he asked. "No, that hurt, we didn't do it that hard," they said. Billy did it again. "You don't know because you were not feeling what she was feeling. I saw the marks you left on her yesterday, and I better never see any more again, understand?"

"Yes, can we go back to our seats now?" they asked.

"No," said Billy. "You two stay back here by yourself, and if you have an urge to hurt someone again, hurt yourself or each other. In fact, if I catch you being a bully to anybody on this bus, then you will answer to me." With that comment, he turned and walked back to where June was sitting. The bus driver began to pull off, she should have already left and perhaps should have come back and stopped Billy, but she didn't. She knew Billy was right in putting a stop to those boys. She had reported them before, but nothing was being done about it. *No harm done*, she thought as she drove off.

Billy thought sure those on the bus would make fun of him for standing up for his little sister and brother. But, the opposite was true. He heard several say to their friends, "I wish my brother would stand up for me like that." Another girl said, "I could really like a boy like that." As Billy sat down beside June, she said, "Thanks." She tried to give him a hug in a way that it would not make him embarrassed before his friends. He whispered to her, "You're welcome. You see, I really do care. I know you sometimes you wish you had a sister, but remember a big brother is always a safe thing to have."

"I know that now," June said with thanks in her voice. She leaned over to look out the window and to ponder about the change that was coming over in her brother. She was really beginning to like him. *Or should I say love him?* she thought to herself. Patrick Henry was not to be left out, jumping into the seat across from them, he said, "Wow! I have this whole seat to myself." They all settled back for the ride to school, which only took about thirty minutes. Arriving at school, they all went to their appointed places.

As Billy stepped off the bus, he was waiting on the side to make sure that everything was OK before he went to class. The driver was the last person off the bus and said to him, "Son, that was a brave thing you did on the bus today. I started to stop it for I will not permit fighting on my bus, however, I saw that those boys respected you and were not going to take you on. If you have any more problems, then please let me know, so as an adult and the driver, I can properly take care of things, deal?"

"Sure," said Billy. "I guess I just acted out of impulse. I was tired of them picking on my sister and brother, and for the record many other kids on the bus. Thanks for understanding I'll let you handle it, if there is a next time."

"Billy, let me give you a challenge, those two boys act like they do because they want attention, they come from a broken home and as best I can tell are latch key kids."

"What's that?" asked Billy.

"That is a term we use for kids who get home to an empty house, no one to look after them or care for them. They go inside and lock the door, or they are supposed to, until a parent gets home. Some single parents, especially mothers, have such a hard time making ends meet that they have to take the best job they can to survive. That does not justify having latch key kids, but it should help us to understand as to why. Here's the challenge I wanted to give you. Those boys know you have gotten their attention, go and do the one thing they least expect you to do."

"What's that?" asked Billy. His mind was racing about all the things he could do to them if they did not stop picking on his family. "Go and be their friend," the driver said.

"What? No way, I don't want those guys for my friends. What would others think.?"

"What is more important, Billy? What would the Lord think? I know that you are a Christian, I've seen that in you, for which I am thankful. As to what your friends would think, what if you were to become a friend and an influence on their lives and they begin to do right, perhaps you could even be used of the Lord to win them to Christ.

"When you give challenges, you give whoppers, I know you are right, and inside I know that in order to overcome your enemies that the best weapon is love. The Bible teaches that where the Lord is honored, then that is where love finds a way. Can I think about it today? I really will pray and ask the Lord what I must do, this is hard, I am only twelve years old and I don't know if I know what to do or how to do it. Remember what you just said, Billy, where the Lord is then, that is where love finds a way. I'll think about it he said as he ran towards class, I'm going to be late if I don't hurry. See you this afternoon he said, as he disappeared into the school building.

"Did he get you in trouble?" said one of his classmates, Freddie, as they rushed down the hall toward class. "No, but as the driver he felt I should let him be the first to take care of a situation like this morning. He actually appreciated what I did, but was concerned about it causing me to become a bully, like those guys have been, or causing a fight, which would end up getting me into trouble. He really did care, and he gave me a challenge to do something, something that I am not sure I can do."

"What's that?" said Freddie, eager to know.

"Can't tell you now," said Billy. "We have got to get in our classroom before the bell rings." Having said that, they both went into the class and found their seats, about thirty seconds before the bell rang. "Cutting it close these morning, boys," spoke the teacher as she called the class to order.

Billy could not make up his mind about school. As he sat at his desk, he heard the teacher and even absorbed what she was saying, but his mind was elsewhere. His school was nice in that everyone knew everyone, for it was the only school in that area for his rural town of Parterre. It had gotten that name for it was located at the central bottom of a beautiful valley in the western part of Virginia. Some say that the Indians named the area and the settlers just adopted the name. *I must check that out sometime*, thought Billy. He had an inquiring mind and if used for good would take him many places. The school was self-governed, in that there was a partnership between the administration for the school and school system, parents, and teachers. What may have been an unusual setup, the school board was made up of an equal balance of representatives from each group, with the president of the board selected by vote among them.

Billy did not understand all of this, he just knew it must work, for the school was successful and the graduates of the school were going places in finding meaningful careers.

One of the things that Billy liked, since he was a Christian, was that there was a freedom to be what you are without someone restraining you. There were others in the school that did not want anything to do with Christian-type programs, but they had learned to respect each other. Instead of fighting, each was giving equal access to what they felt was right for them. The only exception which Billy could think of was last year when some really radical group of boys wanted, under the guise of their equal access, to have a club program that was based on hate and stepping on what others believe. *I know those guys, they wanted a way to get out of class, party and do whatever evil they could, not because of any founded convictions, but because they wanted to get their way at the expense of all others. I am glad they were not allowed to meet alone on campus. What proved to be true is that they began to meet off campus and formed into what they wanted all along, a gang. Some have already been arrested for drinking and drugs and stealing. I am glad they did not let this type stuff in our school. We are here to learn and to prepare ourselves for the future; their hate gave them no future and stifled their learning.*

"Billy," he heard his name being called, and after hearing it the second time he looked up to see the teacher looking directly at him. "Are you going to be part of our class today?"

"Yes, Madame," Billy said. *The teacher was good, she really wanted your attention and would call your name to get it however, and I knew that if she had to call me back to reality again, then she would ask me aside for a conference. She was fair and did not try to use embarrassment as a whip to get the students to behave or be attentive. I appreciate this, for it showed me she really cared and wanted my self-directed attention, not a forced attention to what she was trying to teach us. She allowed the class a few minutes to have their own personal prayers, thoughts, devotion, or just quiet time, as each student felt led. Afterward, we said the pledge of allegiance to the American flag, which I always enjoyed.*

The class progressed as it normally did for the next several hours, until lunchtime. They had several choices for lunch. They could eat at the school cafeteria or they could bring their own lunches. Billy's folks set it up so they could eat in the cafeteria. They felt they would get a better balanced meal and besides considering all the options and hassles of purchasing, making and bringing your own lunch, it worked out financially close to each other. When Billy went to lunch today, he took one of the ham and cheese sandwiches, two cookies, and milk from the selection the cafeteria had. He then went to an outside table. He wanted to be away from others where he could eat in private and think. He had a lot to think about with the challenge given to him. How was he going to do it? He knew it would be right, and he wanted to be alone to also ask the Lord what he should do.

"Lord," Billy began to pray, "only being twelve, how can I do something like this?" As if answering his prayer, his heart reminded him that the Lord Jesus was only twelve went He went to the temple and before the priests and leaders. If Jesus could, by example, do that, why couldn't he? With Jesus in his heart, why couldn't he do this also? Billy had often thought about what the Lord wanted him to do with his life. He really enjoyed the missionaries when they came to his church, but was afraid to say he felt the Lord wanted him to be a missionary because of what others would say. *If I don't do this, and then I know God does not want me to be a missionary,* thought Billy. *OK, I'll do it. But, Lord, please help me.*

Looking around the school grounds, he tried to find the two boys, Tom and Steve, who were twin brothers. He soon found them over by the big oak tree. They were eating their lunch and were all alone, it seemed most of the kids were avoiding them for they had heard what happened on the bus this morning and knew they were just a lot of hot air. Getting up from his seat, Billy began to walk over to them. As he neared, the boys started to get up, not sure what to expect. Billy called out to them, "Stay seated, I just want to talk with you, and I am not going to do anything to you." The boys were not sure, they thought this might be a trick and both of them were ready for whatever. As Billy got near, he sat down beside them and began to speak. "Tom, Steve, I am not sure what I am going to say, and I am not sure exactly why I am here, but hear me out and if you don't like what I say you can get up and walk away, is that a deal?"

"Sure," said Tom first.

"Sometimes we do things because of what is happening in our lives, for example I found out this morning a lot about you both that I did not know."

"Yeah, like what?" asked Steve.

"Nothing bad, so settle down. I found out that you live alone with your mother and that she has to work two jobs to make ends meet. I also feel this is the reason you have been picking on the others for the past couple of months." Tom started to interrupt, but Billy reminded him, "You agreed to hear me out first, right?"

"Sure, go ahead," said Tom. "But I am not sure what you are getting to."

"This is your first year in our school, and you do not know a lot of the other guys. I am only two years older than you guys, which does not make me have all the answers. But I do have some suggestions if you are willing to listen." Both boys looked at each other with puzzled looks on their faces, but said nothing. "Here's the deal, I'm sorry I put you guys down this morning, what you were doing was not right, and doing it to my family really made it personal. What happened this morning and last week and last month is history, what I would like to offer you today, is to be your friend."

"We don't understand," said Tom. "What's the catch?"

"None, no strings attached, I just want to be your friend if you will let me."

"Why you should do that?" said Steve with a doubting voice.

"I was reminded this morning of a responsibility that I have to my sister and brother, but I was also reminded of my responsibility to others. If we could be friends, then we would not have to fight or argue, and I could help you guys get to know others here at school. After school, I have several activities I go to each week, and I am sure I can get you an invitation to come and join us."

"What do you do?" asked Steve.

"On Tuesdays right after school, we meet in the library for a fellowship and Bible study time, after which we play soccer for about forty-five minutes. On Wednesdays I go to church with my folks at 6:30 p.m., and we could pick you up. They have a Wednesday night program for guys our age. It combines games, study, and crafts. Then on Thursdays I meet a bunch of the guys at the sandlot for a softball game. Sometimes my dad takes us fishing or hiking on Saturday, and Sunday morning I go to Sunday school. Friends share, so if you will let me be your friend, then you can go with me to all these things, with your mom's permission of course."

"We heard about those things," said Tom, "but we did not think anybody wanted us there. We saw the bus come by every Sunday for Sunday school, but no one ever stopped at our house to ask if we wanted to go."

"What makes you think they will now?" piped up Steve.

"Because you are my friends, and if they accept me, then they will have to accept you, how about it? I can leave now and no more will be said, and I will not give you guys a hard time, or we can agree to be friends and do things together, choice is yours."

"Yes," they both said with happy voices and Billy almost detected a little wetness in their eyes.

"Well, let's shake on it," said Billy. After shaking hands, they walked and talked together back to class like they had been buddies for a long time, each trying to outtalk the other. The others at school could not believe what they saw and did not understand why Billy wanted to be pals with those guys. However, after a period of time, with Billy helping them, they blended into the group. They had promised Billy they would go to Sunday school with him Sunday, and he said he was going to try to get his dad to pick them up for the first time, and then maybe they could ride the bus after that.

The teacher usually gave the students a fifteen-minute "whatever" as she called it. They could use it for study to review or just for quite time, however, they could not talk. During this time, Billy began to pray within himself, *Lord, that was easy. I don't know how I pulled it off so smoothly.* Then as if he needed to correct his prayer, he said, *Lord, it was easy because you showed me what everyday things could happen when love finds a way. Help me to be a witness and a friend to Tom and Steve, I pray for their salvation. And, Lord, does this mean you want me to be a missionary? Amen.*

The quite time was over, and they completed the last assignment for the day. Leaving the classroom, Billy met Tom and Steve in the hallway. "Are you guys going to sit with me on the bus?" asked Billy. "Sure," they said, still not sure that all this was real. As they walked to the bus, June and Patrick Henry were waiting by the water fountain, they had agreed upon place. They were not happy to see the boys, but had heard rumors during the day that they did not understand. Tom was the first to speak, "Look, we are sorry for how we have picked on you two, and you can be rest assured it will not happen again. Billy has shown us that it is better to be friends than to be bullies." With that, the five of them headed to the bus. The driver was standing at the door, checking them on to make sure he had them all. "Sir," said Billy to him, "these are my friends, Tom and Steve, is it OK for them to sit with me?" He gave the driver a wink, which told him he had taken the challenge. "Get onboard," he said.

Chapter 5

As he got off the bus to go to his class, Patrick Henry was upset. Those boys had scared him and he did not know why they always picked on him. He didn't do anything to them, he thought. He entered the school and ran down the hall to his classroom. When he arrived, his teacher could see he was upset about something, giving him a little extra attention, she asked him to take his seat. For the most part of the morning, Patrick Henry seemed distracted from the rest of the class, not willing to join in and was timid when others yelled at him or confronted him. The teacher noticed this and knew this was not his normal behavior. Something must have happened to him at home or on the way to school. She made a mental note to follow up on this with the first break of the morning. Several times during the class, she said, "I really need some help," hoping Patrick Henry would volunteer. He had always been the first to raise his hand in the past, but not today. That was not working, so the teacher had another plan. Her assistant usually read the class a story each day. This was to get them interested in reading and comprehend what the books were saying. She said, "Class, today we are going to do things a little different. We usually have our story time later in the day, but we will have it now. While the story is being read, I want each of you to sit quite in your seats and listen. I need to go to the storeroom for a moment and let's see. Patrick Henry, would you carry this extra box for me? It's not heavy, but I have my hands full." Patrick Henry got out of his seat to do what the teacher asked. She could tell by the expression on his face that he was not happy to do it.

The teacher and Patrick Henry both left the class, carrying some boxes to the storage area. On the way back, the teacher said, "Patrick Henry, would you mind if we stopped by the office on the way back? I need something." *This was usually where the students were sent who had misbehaved or had to leave notes and things like that,* thought Patrick Henry. When they got into the office, they went into a small office on the right, but no one was there. "Patrick Henry, please have a seat a minute, while the class is finishing hearing the story, I want to talk with you. You are one of the best students I have, and I am really proud of you, did you know that?"

"Nope," said Patrick Henry.

"Come on now, you know you always help me and I can always depend on you. This morning when you came into the class, I noticed that something was wrong, did something happen to you on the bus today?"

"Those boys are picking on me again and they hurt me. I didn't do anything to them, why don't they leave me alone?"

"Where did they hurt you?" she asked.

"See my arm." He showed her. Looking at the arm, she could see a small bruise spot. "Tell you what, we will get the nurse to look at your arm and I will speak to the principal about the boys. Now, you are one of my best students and I need you to perk up and help me with the class."

"Why?" asked Patrick Henry.

"Because you help us have a happy class, will you help me?" responded the teacher.

"Sure," he said. "I'm sorry I was in the dumps. My brother grabbed those boys on the bus this morning and made them sit on the back seat; he told them they would answer to him if they ever touched my sister or me again. They were really scared, and you know sometimes, you think that to your older brother you are just a pest, but Billy showed me he really cares."

"Sounds like you have a wonderful brother, I know of him and he has a good reputation around the school, always helping others, just like you. Now are you going to perk up and help me?"

"Yes, Madam," sounded Patrick Henry in that commanding voice, which for a boy of five could later in life be one, that would lead men, perhaps in the military, thought the teacher. Having seen the nurse who gave his arm some tender loving care, they returned to the classroom, just as the story time was over. "Rats," said Patrick Henry, "I missed the whole story." He took his seat. His classmates knew he was back to being the same old Patrick Henry.

The rest of the day was just a normal day in the K-5 classroom. Patrick Henry, during his quite time in which they took a nap, let his mind wander. He thought, *Maybe one day I will be a policeman, or a fireman, or I will be a soldier like my dad was. I will go off and defend my country.* He wondered, *Does God tell boys my age what they are supposed to do?* Praying within himself, he said, *Lord, thank you for saving me, what do you want me to be? Will you tell me now, or do I have to wait until I am older? My brother, Billy, I know he secretly wants to be a missionary, what do missionaries do? Can I be a preacher just like my pastor? I love him, because I know he loves each of us. Why is my pastor sick? Can you heal him? He really needs to get better. And who will preach on Sunday, can I?* With these thoughts in his mind, he drifted off to sleep. The teacher awakened him as she prepared them for the final lessons of the day.

He really liked his class and his teacher. Most of the boys and girls were like him, he thought, except for this one girl, she never stops talking. She even talks when she is supposed to take her nap, and then there is the boy who cannot sit still. *I bet if they tied him down, that he would wiggle out of it.* He was always getting in trouble, and trouble could find him standing in the middle of the schoolyard. He was always getting dirty, and it took the teacher extra time to clean him up after every outdoor activity. One day, she sits him in a sandbox in the middle of the playground. It was a new sandbox with clean bright yellow sand. *Today he would be clean when he came inside,* thought everyone, and especially hopeful was his teacher. Be it as it may be, as he played in the sand box some birds were flying over the playground and one of them messed, which landed right on top of his head. He went crying to the teacher. "That bird dumped on me," he said. The teacher could not help but have pity on him. He was such a mess. She took him inside, and they cleaned him up as best as they could. It was time for the class to return to their classroom, so the teacher called them all in.

Having completed his handicraft just as the bell rang, Patrick Henry put his things away and went to meet Billy at the water fountain. He was scared to see those boys coming toward them, and he did not understand why Billy was with them. The boys told him they were sorry for picking on him and that it would not happen again, this made him happy. He did not know how this all came about. He remembers his dad saying, "When there are difficulties and there are people that misuse you, then when love finds a way, it will be all right." He was only five, but he knew that it was Billy that found a way, and he hugged his big brother, knowing he was the one who was protecting him. With those thoughts finished, he followed Billy and the boys to the bus.

Chapter 6

Spring was the favorite time of the year of June; she loved to see the flowers and the clover across the fields near her home. She especially loved to see the sunflowers. They were her favorites. She was watching all the beauty of the fields as the bus sped down the highway; at least she was until Tom and Steve started picking on her and Patrick Henry again. She began to cry as they pulled her hair and poked her until it hurt. She was not prepared for what happened next. With no warning, her brother Billy, jumped from his seat, grabbed both boys by their shirts, and forced them to the back seat of the bus. "Leave them alone," she heard him say in a voice that Billy rarely used. He meant business and did not want those ugly boys picking on them. As Billy came back to his seat, June wiped the tears from her eyes and said thanks. "It will be all right, you just watch your pretty flowers in the field, and I'll take care of them." June learned a new respect for her brother that day; she almost regretted her statement at breakfast that she wanted a sister instead of brothers, almost.

Going to school was something that June knew she needed, but she much preferred to live in the country. She wished she had been born in the last century, she felt she would feel more at home. She loved the outdoors and always sought opportunities to be out there. The ride to school was an enjoyable time for her, except when she was being picked on. She would sit next to the window and watch all the beautiful flowers and the budding of spring. She used to count the telephone poles, but after so many times of counting them she gave up on that.

As the bus pulled into the schoolyard, she began to gather her things together in preparation of going to her class. She wanted to get off the bus before those boys did and therefore rushed to be one of the firsts off. As she got off the bus, she saw her brother standing by the door. "It will be all right, sis," said Billy. "Just go on to class." She was glad he cared enough to stay and watch over them. Leaving the bus, she headed to her class.

This past school year had been a difficult one for June. She had gotten into a lot of trouble and seemed to not be able to keep her mind on things. *What's wrong with me?* she thought. She even tried to pray, but that seemed to go nowhere. It was like no one was really there to answer. This day was no different. As she went to her locker, two of the girls in her class began to make fun of her hair, teasing her that she was still just a little girl because she wore double pig tails. The more they made fun of her, the madder she got, and having taken all she felt she should, she went up to one of them and slapped them, saying, "Stop it, stop it, stop it, I'm tired of you two being such brats." The three of them began to argue and slap each other. June was getting the worse of it and could have gotten hurt if it had not been for one of the teacher coming around the corner and seeing what was happening. "You girls stop that right now, now I mean," she repeated when they did not stop. "I want all three of you to the principal's office NOW!" She commanded with an authoritative voice. The girls knew she meant business and that she knew who they were, so they stopped fighting and went to the office. June went slower, letting the other two girls go ahead. She did not want to fight anymore, and she knew she could not win with both of them at the same time.

It seemed like an eternity before the principal called her into his office. They were now all late for class, but then she guessed everyone knew they were there and what had happened. As she entered his office, she did so quietly. She did not want to be there and knew that she was going to be punished. *It wasn't my fault*, she was prepared to say. After about five minutes, the principal and a teacher came into the room. Sitting down, the principal said, "Why don't you tell me what happened, June?"

"Well, I was at my locker, trying to sort my things out for the day when those two girls came and began to make fun of me. They pick on me all the time, today it was my hair. They said I was childish because of how I wore my hair, I happened to like it this way. So today they pushed me too far, and I slapped one of them, then we started to fight. One of the teachers came around the corner, broke it up and made us come here, that's all. And who do those girls think they are? I am not going to do what they do, and they don't like it."

Before she could say any more, the principal interrupted, "June, the one redeeming factor here is that I believe you have told me the truth, you did start the fight by slapping one of the other girls first, is that right?"

"Yes, sir," replied June.

"The others dumped all of the blame on you, which I can understand. They said they had just come up to you to talk, and for no reason at all you slapped them."

"That's not true," cried June, "they were picking on me."

"I understand that, so please calm down, others who saw what happened have already told me that. However, we do have several problems. The first is the fighting. For that, I am asking for your parents to meet with me here at the school. We cannot permit this type of activity, and our school rules state that when blows are given or received, then the parents are asked to come to the school and help us sort out the problem."

"Do we have to?" said June in tone of "I-really-don't-want-to-do-this."

"Yes, it's our rule. The other girl's parents will be asked to come in also. That is just part of the problem, and I believe that it has led us to this happening. The other part is what concerns me most. June, last year you were happy and seemed to really enjoy school and your friends. This year, you seem to be distant and withdrawn. This makes me believe that something is going on in your life that has affected what you do and especially your attitude. Is there anything that you can share with me?" he asked.

"No, sir," replied June, but she said nothing more.

"Would you do me a favor?"

"Sure," said June.

"Would you go and speak with the school nurse? I know you like her and perhaps she can help you sort some things out, that wouldn't be too bad, and you can go now instead of going back to class." *A chance to miss class, great!* thought June. "I'll go," she said. After giving a note for her parents and one for the nurse, he let June leave his office and go to the nurse's office.

Entering the nurse's office was like going into a small medical clinic. She really had some neat stuff. Perhaps one day she would be a nurse, June thought. The nurse had someone with her in the examination room, so she asked June if she would just sit and wait. While she waited, she let her eyes wander over all the medical stuff in the room—no real serious stuff, just things for cuts and bruises, leg wraps, and crutches, and things like that. As she looked with curiosity, the nurse came and asked her to come to her inner office. "The principal seems to think you have got some things on your mind that might be affecting your actions here at school. Now, we have been friends for two years, is that right?"

"Yes, Madam," answered June in a happy voice, she really did like the nurse.

"Well, as friends, could you tell me what's going on?"

"This school year has been different," June began. "When I first got to school, the two girls I had the fight with today tried to be friendly with me. They were new to the school, and I thought that would be good. After a while they wanted me to hang out with them, we went to the mall and stores and things like that. They both kissed a boy one day, the same boy. They said that they were just showing me how to do it; I would have to learn anyhow. They wanted me to kiss the boy and I would not. Later, they said they were just kidding around, besides that boy was much too old for me. They wanted me to go to the mall with them; they said they were going to play hide and find, a game they had made up. What they were really doing was stealing things from the store and putting them in places where they thought no one would look to find. They wanted me to do it also, I was scared. I knew what they were doing was not right and I did not want to do it, and so I didn't. Since then they have picked on me, called me names, and continue to tease me. This morning, I just had it with them and even though I knew I would get beaten up, I hit one of them. Why don't they just leave me alone? Please don't tell my mom and dad or the principal. I didn't do what they did and they are afraid I am going to tell somebody, which I guess I just did," said June with a sad voice.

"When someone wants you to do wrong and you stand up for what is right, that takes courage. June, you are a brave girl. You have taken three months of abuse from these girls for one reason, and you were not going to do wrong. Now I need you to use a little bit more courage and help me help them."

"How do I do that?" asked June.

"Later today, I am going to call them into my office one at a time and confront them with this, for you see I believe that they are having a real problem beyond just what you saw them do, and if someone doesn't help them, it will only get worse. Will you help me?"

"Yeah, what do I have to do?"

"Nothing, you have already done more than enough. I just need to be able to tell them that you told me what was happening and that if they tried to say they didn't do it, then I would ask you to come and say it to their face. I don't believe I will have to call you, but just in case."

"They will beat me up if they know I told you," exclaimed June.

"They are already picking on you now, don't you want that stopped?"

"Yes," said June, "I do, I guess I don't have much choice." After speaking with June for a few more minutes to reassure her that she had made the right choices and that things will work out all right, she sent June back to the class.

During the break time, the girls came over to June. "You spent a long time with the principal, what did you say, did you tell him anything?" They commanded to know. "No I did not." It was true, she did not speak to him. "Thanks to you I have a note to have my parents come to the school and I was sent to the nurse's office, it's your entire fault and I hate you," said June as she ran away from them and back into the classroom. With the teacher in the classroom, she felt safe sitting at her desk and reading a book. The rest of the day went as usual, and when the last bell rang, June gathered all of her stuff. Having already decided to not stop at her locker, she went directly for the water fountain, where she hoped Billy would be there. When she arrived, Patrick Henry was there. "Where's Billy?" she asked. "Here he comes," said Patrick Henry, "I see him on the walkway." Turning, June saw him, but those bad boys were with him, why, she didn't understand and was afraid. As they approached them, Tom said they were sorry for picking on them and that it would not happen again. June was not sure what had happened or how Billy pulled this off, but she was glad and got on the bus. Taking her usual seat, she wanted to see the sunflowers on her way home. They were at full stalk and looked good enough to eat.

Chapter 7

As the bus traveled the road, June was able to see her sunflowers. Patrick Henry watched the skies for planes, and Billy talked with his new friends. The bus ride seemed short this time because of all of the interesting things each had seen or done. The boys, who were the first of the new set of friends to get off the bus, said goodbye to Billy, June, and Patrick Henry. The boys' stop was a few more miles down the road. As the bus drove off, the three of them walked to the house. Billy stopped to get the mail, which was his job; Patrick Henry hoped one day he could do it. Having gotten the mail, they walked and into the house, and as their usual practice they went directly into the kitchen, hoping to find their fresh milk and snack.

As expected, Mom's in the kitchen, putting the final touches on their coming home snack. This was something they all looked forward to; it was like a family tradition. "Mom," Billy said, "I'm really glad that you are here when I come home each day. I know a lot of kids who know don't have anyone waiting for them, and that is really sad."

"Yeah," said June, "I feel the same, it's great that you care for us like you do. I guess that when you want to, 'love does find a way every day.'"

Jay and Bill were just getting off work and heading toward the parking lot. As they approached the car, Jay asked, "How was your day, Bill?"

"Just great," replied Bill. "I just cannot believe how much difference my day at work was, I really enjoyed my job today. I am usually a loner and not very easy to get along with, but today it was different. I know that being a Christian must be the difference. I see things in a different perspective; I find joy in what I am doing and in the people I am around. I find myself liking people and while I am basically a shy person, I just cannot believe my boldness in sharing my newfound faith with others. I just know that what the Lord has done for me has given me hope and a new perspective on life."

"I know what you are feeling, Bill," said Jay. "I haven't gotten over that feeling all the years I have been a Christian, and I hope you do not either. Just put Christ first in your life and you will find victory day by day. As you have found, 'Love makes a way every day.'" With those comments, they had arrived at Bill's home.

"See you tomorrow, Bill, same time and same place."

"Thanks, Jay," said Bill. "Keep me in your prayers. I will need them as I try to do what is right." With those comments, Bill drove away heading toward home with a glad heart and a renewed joy in seeing a new Christian and the blessing of having placed his faith in the Lord. Bill could not wait to share the blessings of today with his family. He would soon get that chance, for he was now driving into his driveway. The boys were playing ball in the lot beside the house, and June was sitting on the porch with a sad look on her face. Just as Bill stepped on the porch, Nell came out the front door and into Bill's arms. "Glad to see you home, husband," she said and gave him a big kiss.

"Is this special treatment or do I sense a question coming on?"

"Can't a wife show her husband she loves him without him questioning?"

"Sure she can," said Bill, "and anytime you want to."

"How was your day, June?" asked Dad.

"It could have been better," replied June.

"Anything we should talk about?" Mom asked.

"Well yes, I guess we do need to talk about a few things that happened to me today, but can we do that at our family time? If I have to talk, then I want it to be family time for what I have to say needs to be said before everyone."

"Wow, that was some statement, June," replied Dad. "We are available to talk with you if you want us to, however, if you want to wait until our family time tonight then that is OK too."

"Yeah, I do," said June.

"Then family time it is," said Mom, as she called everyone into the house for supper.

The meal was great as usual. *Mom must be the best cook in town*, thought Patrick Henry. Maybe he should invite some of his friends over so they can taste her great cooking. With the evening meal done and the dishes put away, each of the children went to their rooms to do their homework or personal study. This was the usual habit of their family, especially on a school night. As the night passed on, the clock chimes rang out fairly loud at eight o'clock. It seemed to be louder than usual, Perhaps the clock was calling them all together for family time, a special time for victory and sharing that each would have a part in. Without suspecting or planning, they had each in their own separate way discovered during their daily routine that "love made a way" in each of their lives in a special way, this day.

Their family time was usually held in the living room, and this time Patrick Henry was the first to arrive with June and Billy racing to see who would be second. Mom and Dad were already in the room where she and Jay had been discussing some of their personal events of the day. "Did the clock chime louder or was that my imagination?" said June. "It sounded much louder," said Billy. "Maybe it knows that I have something special to share at our family time tonight."

"Me too," said both June and Patrick Henry at the same time. Mom showed more surprise on her face than did Dad, and was the first to speak. "Dad, if we can have our opening prayer, then I am eager to see what our children have to share about their day today."

"Me too," said Dad. "I have much to share also, lets pray." Having led the family in a brief prayer, Dad said, "For tonight, let's do two things. It seems everyone has something to share about what the Lord has shown them today, so if we need to, Patrick Henry you can stay up till ten if we need that much time."

"Great," said Patrick Henry.

"Tonight we will do things a little different, lets share what we have and then end our family time with the Word and prayer. We will start on my left and go around the room, each of you share something about what the Lord has shown you today. June, you are the closest to my left, so you start first."

"Well," began June, "today was a difficult day for me. I am not sure where to start or how to say what I have to say, so I will just say it as it comes to my mind and hope everyone can sort out the details. My day started off as it usually does with the boys on the bus picking on me. However, for some reason, my brother Billy came to the rescue and put those boys in their place. I saw what he did on the bus, and he really scared those guys. I am not sure what he did afterward, but when those boys came up to me in the hallway at school, they told me they were sorry for what they had done and would not be doing it again. They were also friendly and nowhere near what they had been before. That was the good news, now for the bad. I got into trouble today at school. Mom, you know the girls that I told you about that had been picking on me? Well, we kind of got in a fight today because I was tired of them picking on me, so when they started it again, I slapped them both. We began exchanging slaps when a teacher came up and took us to the principal. The principal asked me what had happened, and I told him the truth. He really knew most of the story anyway and since he knew I was telling the truth, he did not punish me, but the school rules say you have to come for a meeting with him. Here is a note from him." Before anyone could say anything, June continued. "That is not all! I guess I should share the real reason why the girls are picking on me. After they first got to our school, I thought it would be cool to hang out with them and be a friend to them. I soon found out that was not a good idea. They kept wanting me to kiss a boy, so I could learn how, and they also planned a game they made up when they went to the mall called 'pick and hide.' The game meant you pick something up in the store and hide in places under you dress where you think most people would not suspect and not dare to touch you. In other words, they were shoplifting. While it was cool being with them when they were not doing bad things, I did not want the things I knew were not right to do. Since I broke off being with them, they have picked on me, mostly to keep me quite so I would not tell on them. The school nurse talked to me today and I shared this with her, she is a good friend and I felt would not only listen but also help. She is going to confront the girls with it and see if she can help them."

"Wow!" was all that that Patrick Henry could say with an expression on his face that seemed to make his eyeballs bulge out. Mom started to say something just as Dad did and backed off, saying, "You go first, dear."

"June, what have you learned from this?" asked Dad.

"The most important thing I learned was that it is always right to do right. I was only hurting myself by keeping all these problems within me when I should have shared them with the Lord and with my family. I thought that I was the one in the wrong, and the more I fought the problem the more I stopped praying and reading my Bible. I was really getting away from the Lord because I was not sure He would love me or if you would love me if you found out. Now I know that was wrong and that through it all I know that God's love will find a way as I know your love will also. Right now, I really need to ask the Lord to forgive me, and also my family for not sharing with them what was bothering me and making me moody and hard to get along with. Will you forgive me?"

Mom spoke, "Why don't we bow our hearts and heads and you speak with the Lord about His forgiveness, for we certainly do."

With that comment, June prayed and asked the Lord to forgive her for not trusting in Him more and for letting her family down. At the end of the prayer, all added, "Lord, we forgive her also."

"June, thank you for sharing this with us. I wish you had come sooner as it would have allowed us to help you carry a burden. We may do that which we choose to do, but it is up to someone to determine the consequences. At this point, I believe that is your principal's responsibility. We will make an appointment to see him this week and sort this out."

"Yes, Dad," replied June. Sad because she had to face the consequences, but happy that she had shared this with her family and their love had found a way to forgive her and help her.

"My turn," piped up Patrick Henry. "My day started off like June's on the bus, but Billy took care of that. I was really sad in class and was not helping my teacher like I normally do. The teacher asked me to go and help her carry a box to the storeroom, but I think it was a trick to get me out of the room and I missed the story time. I always enjoy the story time. I was right, the teacher asked me to tell her what was making me so sad. At first I did not want to, but then I did. I was not happy because of the boys picking on me. She said that she had heard rumors of the boys picking on others also and for me not to fret as she was going to check on it. I told her what Billy had done, but I did not know what he did during the day because when I got out of class, the boys were by the water fountain. That is where Billy and June and I met every day before we get on the bus. The boys were there with Billy, and they were acting like old buddies. As I came up to the fountain, Tom, the older of the twins by three minutes, told me he was sorry for what he had been doing and that he and his brother were not going to pick on us again. Wow, that was something else. I guess that when love finds a way, it really works."

"Well, Billy, it seems as if you are the hero for the day!" explained Dad.

"Not really," said Billy. "I just did what I should have done in the first place. If anybody is going to pick on my sister and brother, then it ought to be me. The bus driver saw me take those two boys to the back of the bus and tell them that if they messed with June or Patrick or any of the other kids on the bus again, they would answer to me. I don't know why I did it, I just did. I guess that when you love someone like your sister and brother, that is when love finds a way for you to do what is right. As we got off the bus, the driver stopped me. I thought he was going to turn me into the principal and fuss at me, but he did not. He said he had heard and saw the whole thing, and since I had not hit them, he felt that it had done more good than harm, however I should let him handle these matters in the future. I told him I would. He also told me why the boys acted as they do. They just want attention. They are latchkey kids and do not have anyone to care for them as their mom works many hours of the day just to make things go for them. The driver challenged me to make friends with them. I did not want to do that, as I really did not like them. But I told him I would pray about it. During lunchtime, I did that. I asked the Lord to show me how to do what I did not want to do but knew I should do. Before the lunchtime was over, I went over to the boys and told them straight out that I knew about them and did not want any more trouble, as I wanted to be their friend. I told them if they would be my friends, then I would invite them to do some of the things I do. They agreed and they even want us to pick them up for Sunday school this Sunday, can we, Dad?"

"Sure," Dad said. "That would be great!"

"They can ride the bus after the first Sunday, but I thought it would be better if they went with us first. Also something else happened, which I am not really sure about or how to say it, so here goes. For some time now, I have been praying about what the Lord wanted me to do and I secretly have wanted to be a missionary. Somehow as I was talking to the Lord, I felt that if He helped me succeed in winning over the boys as friends, then I could also win others for Christ. And He really did help me. I was amazed at how easy it was to make friends with the boys. They just wanted someone to show them that love can find a way for them also. Dad, how do I tell others that the Lord wants me to be a missionary?"

"Well," said Dad, "why not go forward at church this Sunday in the morning service and just tell the pastor what you just told us. You make the step forward and then let the Lord fill in the rest of the pieces."

"OK, I will do it," said Billy.

Everyone else said, "Amen!"

"Wow!" said almost everyone.

"This is a really special day for all of us. Mom has not shared yet, so let's hear what she has to say."

Jill began by sharing about her visit with Sally and then how the Lord had used her all day to teach others and to confirm in her heart that she really needed to be serving the Lord by teaching. "Some of the men and ladies from the church had gone to Sally's house and fixed it all up really nice, western style, which is what she likes. She is from out west. If you could see what they did to Sally's house and how much love they put into helping her and Sally's also coming to know Christ as her personal Savior, then you would understand the glow I hope I have. The folks at our church really went so far in helping that it was clear how love had found a way to be a blessing. One more thing, she is about to have her baby. I believe she is in her eighth month. I offered for her little boy to come and stay with us while she go to the hospital and until she is back on her feet. He is five just like Patrick Henry."

"Can he stay in my room with me?" piped up Patrick Henry, like his old self again.

"Sure, he can," said Mom. "Now for the rest of the story!

I felt so strong about the teaching part, that when I went by the church to drop off some of the preserves for the pastor and missionaries' families, I shared with the pastor how the Lord was dealing with me about teaching. I told him I was willing to teach any class, but preferred the fifth grade."

"Jill," Bill spoke up, "we are really so proud of you and know you will not only be a good teacher but will be very happy in doing so."

"Finally, it's my turn," said Dad. "As you know I have been praying for Bill, the fellow that rides with me, to get saved. I had tried to witness to him but knew that because of something that happened to him a long time ago that I needed to be available and not be pushy. Bill went home to visit his folks last week, and while he was there, he met a high school girl he had a crush on. Mary was her name. Bill said that Mary was different; he was not sure what it was, just different. Mary had become a Christian, and her faith was shown through her mannerism and smile. I won't share all the details but Bill did accept the Lord and now I have a new Christian brother and share rider in my car. When we allow the Lord to work in our hearts, we certainly can say that in all things, when love finds a way we can see the blessings of the Lord. We have all had a full day of blessings and I can think of no greater time for us to pray and thank the Lord that His love found a way for each of us in our own circumstances this day, let's pray . . ."

"I will walk before the Lord in the land of the living." (Psalms 116:9)

Post Note: I was greatly inspired in my Christian life by the book *In His Steps* by Shelton. It was the inspiration of that book that led me to pen *Where Love Finds a Way*. In each step of our lives, in each decision we make, if we base every decision on how we feel the Lord would best want us to do what we are about to do, go where we are planning to go, or say what we feel we should say, then acting upon that decision based on Christ living within, we can only find success in our Christian lives. My prayer for you as you have read this book is that love for Christ and love for others will find a way in and through your life.

About the Author

Dr. Painter is a retired naval officer earning twenty-two decorations with multiple citations, and he was decorated by all four services while serving three tours in Vietnam and an 80 percent service connected disabled veteran. His service started with the Florida National Guard, then the US Navy as enlisted for eleven years when he earned a commission rising the Navy rank of lieutenant. He joined the US Airforce Auxiliary Civil Air Patrol in 1998 raising to the rank of Chaplain Lt. Colonel. He is currently assigned as the Florida Deputy Wing Chaplain for the USAF Auxiliary Civil Air Patrol.

As an American Indian elder who works with tribal groups throughout the South East. He serves as an advisor for the Mayo Clinic Rochester Spirit of Eagles American Indian Program, executive elder for the South East American Indian Council, Inc., recruiting and training community health workers (CHW) to serve in tribal villages, and he conducts needs assessment researcher for NACR and NACI. He has conducted sole contracts for the State Board of Health for Florida, Georgia, and South Carolina for health initiatives among

American Indians for cancer, diabetes, and tobacco cessation. He lectures at national, regional, and state medical conferences on cancer, diabetes, and disparities of heath care among minorities and served on the CHW Certification Council to certify CHW workers in the state of Florida.

He has several earned bachelor and master's degrees with earned doctorate degrees in management science, education, and family and marriage counseling. He is an NCCA certified professional counselor. He is past president and chancellor of two universities and two colleges and is currently mentoring chancellor of Taongi National University.

He founded Mission Harvest America Inc. and for 27 years serving as CEO, directing the organization's international humanitarian aid and disaster relief, which supplied over 216 million pounds of donated relief materials valued at over $185,000,000.00, shipping, (8,775 plus) sea containers in support of global activities in 70 countries and 47 States within the USA.

As an instructor level post-graduate university professor, he has been directly involved in starting colleges and universities in Romania, Liberia, Africa, and the USA, and establishing orphanages and secondary educational systems in various countries. Additionally, he serves as a member or chairman of ten boards of directors from research, to education, and ministry. He serves at the Falcon Chapter of the Air Force Association and past president of the Optimist Club of Jacksonville. He is the executive director of the International Education Professional Accreditation Association and has published several books and currently working on four new manuscripts. Dr. Painter can be contacted by writing him at Post Office Box 551065, Jacksonville, Florida 32255-1065.